Free to Be Good or Bad

*the text of this book is printed
on 100% recycled paper*

Herbert Holt, M.D.

FREE TO BE GOOD OR BAD

BARNES & NOBLE BOOKS

A DIVISION OF HARPER & ROW, PUBLISHERS

New York, Hagerstown, San Francisco, London

Contents

PART ONE. **The Great American Daydream**

    1. Psychoplastics or the Perfect Nose   3
    2. Magic-Think   15
    3. Whither the Pop Therapies?   31

PART TWO. **Hotlines to Nowhere**

    4. Me, Myself, and I   53
    5. Out of This World   77
    6. The Rose-Garden Children   101

PART THREE. **The Existential Road**

    7. In Defense of Uniqueness   121
    8. The Culture Dream   144
    9. The Art of Renegotiation   165
    10. Free to Be Good or Bad   187

The Great
American Daydream

I

Psychoplastics
or the Perfect Nose

1

The hippies are now married and have ten-year-old children, nostalgia for a romantic past is in fashion, and yet the pendulum of social change still swings erratically. Psychotherapy, once for the few and now for the many, looks more and more like the cosmetic and entertainment industries.

A woman came into my office for a consultation. "Doctor," she said, "you must help me. What I want is really very little. I only want a new nose."

She had been to three plastic surgeons, and all had

refused her. She wanted me to find her a fourth.

I looked at her nose. It was a bit long, a bit humped, not a Greek nose, rather a Roman one, but it suited her strong-featured face and I told her so. She brushed my comment aside. What she wanted was not an antique Greek or Roman but a Hollywood contemporary sex-queen style of nose, no matter whether it went with the rest of her face. She exclaimed passionately, "You must understand! A new nose will give me a new personality, it will open new worlds to me, it will bring me a new man, a wonderful new life!"

Of course, no reputable plastic surgeon will take a patient with such expectations.

This woman may not be representative but she is symbolic. Countless thousands of Americans line up at the counters of the therapy department store, looking for a psychic new nose that will change their lives. And behind the counters stand the merchants of fantasy, each extolling his own brand of packaged psycho-plastics. I do not blame the merchants. Most of them are perfectly sincere. They believe in their own therapies.

Regularly each week, for one or several treatment sessions, the hopeful seekers arrive at a plush-carpeted studio, a windowless bare loft, a psychic spa with heated swimming pool, an ordinary apartment house living room, or an office equipped with the traditional couch.

For the therapy shoppers also crowd the sanctums of the traditional psychotherapy schools. Papa Freud is long since dead and buried, but for some there is still hope at the shrine of St. Sigmund or one of his many and various disciples. The shoppers sample Freudian, Jungian, Adlerian, Horneyan varieties or mixtures thereof. They sniff the treatment like some lotion or moisturizing cream, looking for wonders to come out of jars of custom-blended words and revelatory silences, and when the wonders do not arrive on schedule they move on.

Every year I see as patients the refugees from touch-and-feel, biofeedback, hypnotherapy, astrology, graphology, palmistry, and Tantra retreats. I see escapees from sedation therapy, hallucinotherapy, scream therapy, sensitivity marathons, short-cut psychoanalyses, sex clinics. Young men and young women report their orgasmic scores on the naïve assumption that total sexual freedom will unravel their emotional kinks and guarantee them a pain-free life of glamorous adventure. Well, I tell them, schizophrenics also register a very high sexual potency.

These seekers approach psychotherapy as they would a beauty salon or slimming spa. They come to have their psyches shampooed, touched up, teased, primped. They look for a dainty psychological scalpel that will painlessly remove the mole, the wart, the single unfortunate personality trait. If only that one little defect can be doctored, fixed, removed, then the world is their paradise, an Eden without a serpent.

Temporarily it works, whatever the treatment. For

a while they look and feel better. Like the man in the television commercial who splashes after-shave lotion on his face to wake him up, they enjoy a brief euphoria. But after the therapeutic tinctures and creams have been well rubbed in, after the delights of leaping on the grass, bathing in the nude, and liberated sex have faded, then they lapse again into discontent, perhaps even deeper with each disappointment. And they are off on another shopping tour, seeking a different "course," a more charismatic guru.

Psychic Service Stations

What an extraordinary notion this is, that a human psyche can be doctored up the way the automobile mechanic doctors up your car with a tightening of connections here, an adjustment there, a change of oil and perhaps a new part, all in a few hours with the right technical skill. The self is that most individual product of inheritance and environment, developed through a long maturing during which it learns its own identity as separate from parents, siblings, friends. That this unique entity can be taken into the machine shop of some quick therapy and tinkered with like the product of an assembly line—is this not a ludicrous illusion?

True, human beings are the most adaptable of living species, often too adaptable for our own good—we can learn to live with almost anything. It is also true that we learn to change ourselves, to modify our behavior, our attitudes, if purely for survival. We learn this from the moment we utter our first cry, and if we live with conscious awareness we continue to learn it throughout life. But this conscious awareness of ourselves, of our separate and unique individuality, we learn only through our daily interaction with the unique and individual selves of the others who share our lives.

No, you will never find yourself in exotic therapies or encounter groups, however charismatic the guru—all you will find there is a laboratory artifact of yourself. We physicians know that what works *in vitro* does not necessarily work *in situ*—what looks like a breakthrough in the test tube may well fizzle out in the application. Animals in the zoo are not the same as in nature, and even atomic particles behave unnaturally in the laboratory, or so the nuclear physicists tell us.

You will not find yourself by seeking in artificial places. People find themselves only in the interaction with other people, and only in the genuine encounters of actual living.

We discover who we are and what we are in no other way than by experiencing ourselves *over and against* the other, in both harmony and disharmony. And the more genuinely we experience the uniqueness of the other, the more profoundly we recognize our own. There is no laboratory or test tube substitute for this intensely human experience of ourselves. It comes to us only through each other.

And the proof of this is the very fact that people keep therapy shopping lists, and go about sampling one system after another—because in none of them do the seekers find what they are looking for.

For too long, therapists have acquiesced to the demands of patients to have their unbecoming traits made over—to walk out with perfect noses. In such a climate of expectation, therapists have come to be viewed—and some to view themselves—as wonder-workers, psychic perfectionizers.

Some therapists have come to believe with their clients that the human personality is necessarily an unfinished, half-baked product like a brown-and-serve dinner roll. And why shouldn't they, when people come to them as one young woman in her twenties came to me, saying, "I know my parents spoiled me, and I don't hold it against them—but fix it for me, Doctor, fix what they did wrong."

Abracadabra—and out comes the psychic panacea like the rabbit out of the hat.

I do not denigrate the patients who come in anguish, suffering real ills of mind or body, seeking ways to deal with failed hopes and unfulfilled dreams, rejection, isolation, distress born of misunderstanding of themselves and the world. Life is not easy on this troubled planet. Many people go about their daily lives competently but joylessly, and many harbor deep angers at memories of injuries past and present, real and imagined. Bitter dialogues, never uttered, buzz like hornets in their heads. They cry easily because they are indeed in pain. But the therapy shoppers are not usually seeking relief from deep-seated, unrelenting pain. They are seeking relief from dullness and discontent. Their discontent is with their daily lives—which often are, in fact, dull and unsatisfying—but they turn it against themselves. They are restlessly, irritably dissatisfied with themselves. They dream of emerging radiant and reborn out of the therapeutic beauty salon.

Who would quarrel with such dreams? Who has not dreamed of being reborn a prince or princess, immune to grief, to illness, to ill fortune, who brings only goodness, joy, and beauty to share with all? The whole human race has dreamed such dreams, and we inherited them as children in our folk and fairy tale books.

But if they seek to make such dreams come true with some magical new therapy, the shoppers are doomed to disappointment. A therapist is not a fairy godmother or a Faustian Mephistopheles. A therapist is more like the Wizard of Oz, warm-hearted, well-meaning, more or less skillful and ingenious but not possessed of any magical powers.

On the other hand, if the shoppers knew what they are really shopping for, they would not be disappointed. What they are seeking is a fantasy trip, an escape from the limitations of their daily lives. They want a journey to the moon, a holiday in some seductive never-never land, a vacation from reality. Why not?

I agree with a colleague of mine who has called this

the Age of Therapies, but only if by therapies we mean entertainments. The therapy seekers go from one to another, stay with each as long as it continues to entertain, then go on to the next, as holiday seekers go from one cruise to another, one vacation resort to another. There are vacation clubs on romantic tropical beaches that offer total escape from reality, where the guests spend all day in bathing suits and never need to think of time or money from the moment they arrive until they leave.

Unfortunately, most of the people who mistake entertainment for therapy do not seek it in a holiday spirit. They seek it frantically. They are looking not for temporary escape but for permanent salvation.

This is not new—it has happened before. There was a time in the Middle Ages when hordes of adults and children left their homes and went wildly dancing through the towns and villages until they dropped. They were seeking to escape from a real terror, the terror of the plague, the Black Death. Some of them, the flagellants, beat themselves until they bled, to drive out the evil that would bring on them the punishment of the plague. We can be sure that even those therapies were successful for some, especially the young and hardy.

Some who seek salvation in one of the modern therapies seem to find it. They attach themselves to it, surround themselves with others who are equally attached to it, and make of it a way of life. This also is nothing new. In ancient times there were the Eleusinian mysteries, the Dionysian rites, and the cult of Mithras, which bathed its initiates in the blood of the sacrificial victim. Those also were entertainments, although sometimes of a grisly kind, but they were only for the initiated, the elect. People who find happiness in feeling themselves the elect of a cult are surely at liberty to do so, but one wonders why they feel compelled to call it a therapy.

Some who seek not therapy but a holiday may find that it comes at quite a high price, as one young couple discovered. They neither needed nor wanted therapy. Theirs was a blissful union. Their friends called them the Sams, as though the two had dissolved into a single human entity. They did everything together, sat together at parties, echoed each other's opinions and each other's jokes.

One day a friend suggested that they might spend part of their vacation at an encounter retreat, just for the experience and the fun. There they met another couple of the same age and tastes. In the whirl of erotic undercurrents and the subtle persuasions of the leader toward self-liberation, the two couples succumbed to the titillations of a change of partners. When their stay was ended they took a cottage in the vicinity and continued their *ménage à quatre*. Then, vacation over, they returned home.

But the Sams, once so happy together, felt ill at ease with each other, and soon they were sexually estranged. Suddenly, the wife left home and husband to join the male member of the other couple. Bereft and lonely, the remaining Sam took unscheduled leave from his job and followed her, presumably to take up where he had left off with the other wife. But now there was nothing in the relationship for either of them, and soon after the double divorce it appeared that there was nothing between Mrs. Sam and the other husband, either. So two happy couples became four miserable, lonely individuals. It was Mrs. Sam who came to me for treatment, looking ravaged and dazed as though she had just walked away from a terrible automobile accident.

I have heard it said that these popular therapies are simply a new fad, and that they will go away. But they are not new. They are humanity's oldest ways of dealing with pain and anguish, whether of the body or the mind. They go back to ancient Mesopotamia, to Ur of the Chaldeans, and they were already old when Father Abraham was born there.

There is nothing new in a therapeutic course called Mushrooms, Meditation, and Massage, recently offered by a popular center, except perhaps the packaging. And some of the ancient incantations of the past must have sounded much like the therapeutic vocalizations heard today in sleek salons, which hopeful patients pay in inflated dollars to learn.

These therapies will not go away, because they have never gone away. Neither the rational Greeks nor the stern Church fathers could get rid of them. They have gone in and out of fashion and sometimes they have gone underground but they have always been with us.

What surprises me is that so many people are disappointed in them, because in ancient times they seem to have been successful. Grateful patients left vast numbers of votive offerings at the healing shrines—to the delight of the archaeologists—and some of the offerings were both beautiful and costly.

Perhaps the modern guru would be more successful if he followed the ancient prescriptions more precisely. Perhaps, like a proper Chaldean physician, he should wear a turban and embroidered caftan, ride an onager, which is a Mesopotamian ass, and consult not only the stars but the flight of birds and the liver of a freshly killed sheep. That would surely add authenticity and it might even contribute to the therapeutic effect.

The question today is, What kind of therapy? Instant relief from boredom, which is perceived as a kind of sickness? Or cure? And if cure, from what?

I have never cured anyone.

Then what happens?

They get better.

- *If you don't know the self you are looking for, how will you know when you've found it?*

- *A slimming spa is no place for reducing emotional bulge.*

- *In an artificial setting, all you can see is the make-up.*

- An individual in an encounter group is no more like his real self than a drunk at a party.

- A therapist cannot wipe away personality blemishes; only a poor therapist would leave his patient so bereft.

- Looking for your self by yourself is like looking into one of a pair of facing mirrors. Nothing new is revealed and the image, at first multiplied, merely vanishes into infinity.

- You and I have no individuality, no reality, except in relation to each other.

Magic-Think

2

People get better because they become educated—from the head down, not from the crotch up. They get better when they find their way out of the cluttered room of childhood fantasies, of false expectations, of cultural imprisonment, of the shared neuroses of our times. I merely act as an informed escort service.

But the resistance is powerful against having one's sights turned toward existential reality and away from the papier-mâché landscape of dreams. People cling to hopes of shortcuts to cure where there is no cure—because there is no sickness, only discontent and boredom.

Boredom is not a sickness. It is an inevitable part of the human condition. We have only to remember the tedium of court life in the palaces of Europe, the boredom of the leisure class, the ennui of the German intellectuals that led them into the extravagances of Romanticism, even to suicide. When the lower animals are not hunting for food or a mate or escaping from their predators, they sleep. But human beings long ago learned to keep awake and use their superior intelligence for invention and creation. And this is a mixed blessing, because the farther we are removed from the edge of survival, the more difficult it is to fill our waking leisure with productive occupation, and even the work most of us do for a living has little trace of either inventiveness or creativity.

And what can come out of boredom except discontent? People are discontented with their lives, with themselves as they are. They look for ways to have the wrinkles ironed out of their personalities, to have new and improved ingredients piped into their character structure, the way the manufacturers put new ingredients—magic whiteners, instant spot removers—into their detergents.

To meet the demand, the exotic new therapies have multiplied like supermarket cleansing powders, and they have even been exported around the world. In France the sensitivity training movement is called *Le T group,* a bit of Franglais like *le drugstore,* and in Japan it is known as Western Zen. The traditional therapies as well have proliferated, rabbitlike, into orgon therapy, rational therapy, conditioned-reflex therapy, directive therapy, nondirective therapy, and most recently one called esthetic realism, a subcult that promises we shall all live beautiful lives if only we know what the true essence of beauty is.

Who are the consumers of these new and improved brands? One investigator found that encounter consumers are a remarkably diversified lot that includes computer programmers, cattle tycoons, black militants, stockbrokers, ex-convicts, psychologists, dancers, clergymen, the idle rich, and the disenchanted poor. On the shopping list are special courses for kleptomaniacs, bisexuals, dentists, ambassadors, admirals, corporation presidents, secretaries, and stewardesses. In an encounter version of Gestalt therapy, opposites are confronted with each other—cops with criminals, socialites with ghetto children, blacks with whites. On the premise that more is better, there has developed a population of encounter freaks, people who have become addicted to these group rituals and who, perhaps, may one day begin mugging and purse-snatching for the price of a "fix" at some therapy center.

There are therapies for normal people who suffer no pain whatsoever, apparently on the assumption that if you are normal a little therapy will render you more normal and a lot of therapy will make you a superstar of normality. In the therapy market you can find a course to fix anything you want fixed, from low sexual capacity to falling hair. You can find therapies to correct social awkwardness, shyness, blushing, remedies for premature ejaculation, relief for intellectuals who think too much and so have forgotten how to get in touch with their feelings and especially with their crotches where, as one guru expressed it, "all the action is."

What this mass movement toward therapy tells us is that there is a massive revival of the ancient exercise of magical thinking. Throughout man's history, therapy and magic have gone together like lox and bagels or fish and chips. Indeed, magic and medicine were originally one and the same thing, whether for physical or for mental ills. Medicine was magic practiced by a tribal elder, a talented shaman, and in more advanced cultures by a priest of the prevailing religion. The ancient Egyptians chiseled an opening in the patient's skull to let out the demon that was causing him mental torment. I hestitate to recommend such a drastic therapy today, but from the evidence of the mummies, some did recover from classic craniotomies and some even had the treatment more than once. Where the demons went after their escape, history does not say, but occasionally I recognize one or two coming out of a patient's mouth.

Living by Magic

I do not put down magic. It is by no means an inferior ingredient of the human psyche. Magic was an enormous advance in mankind's development, the third great step after toolmaking and language. By means of magic, he emerged from a half-erect animal, scarcely more intelligent than his fellow primates, into a cognitive being, capable of reasoning, of abstract thought, of creative imagination. Magic was the beginning of art, religion, science, and philosophy; the parent seed of intellect.

At its birth, magic saved the human species from helplessness and perhaps from extinction. In the face of the terrors of his environment, which today we are only beginning to understand, the magical beliefs of early man gave him explanations for lightning and thunder, for earthquake and volcano and devastating forest fires, for the dangerous animals against which he had neither tooth nor claw but only his own puny strength and the inventions of his creative mind.

Magic explained to him the mysteries of birth, death, his own existence, and his sleeping dreams. Magic gave him a sense of power. It gave him the courage to live another day, in a harsh and dangerous world that in no way resembled the paradisaical Eden of our beautiful and inspiring mythology, which itself is a creation of magical thinking.

Like early man, when we are baffled and helpless in the face of what is going on around us and inside of us, we are sorely tempted to resort to magical thinking. Jean Piaget in his explorations of children's minds found that they, too, had magical explanations of things and events, very close to those of early mankind. Children feel small and helpless in a world of giant adults and unpredictable events, and magic is their tool to cope with their world, to give them a sense of power and control.

This yearning for an explanation and—even more—for a little bit of power over what happens to us, stays with us into adulthood. We all crave certainty. We all long for a peek at the bottom line.

Magic is a precious gift, a spur to creativity and an enrichment of our daily lives in dream and fantasy. But it has its limitations. A prehistoric hunter facing an enraged mastodon may have gained courage from the magic of his cave painting, which guided his spear to the heart of the great animal. But it was his sharp eye and unerring arm, the hunter's skill born of effort and experience, that alone could bring down the huge beast. Magic is not a substitute for hard-earned skill and hard-headed intelligence in dealing with reality.

Magic, like many great gifts, is neutral, neither good nor evil in itself but only in the way we use it. It can be a boon or a curse, and when it is abused it becomes dangerous. Many young people, still under the spell of childhood magic, live as though they were impervious to disaster, as though accident or failure can happen only to others, never to them.

I have in mind a young man, a patient, who fell into a suicidal depression when he failed in an examination that would have won him entrance to medical school.

He had copped out on his studies for years—through high school, through college—counting on his facility and genuine brilliance to get him through. And, then, with his belated discovery of a vocation, he applied himself for three months, confident that he could prepare in that time for an examination for which others studied for three years. True, he was gifted—his IQ was well up to genius level—but only a magical belief in his gifts would have persuaded him that he could summon complex biochemical formulas out of his mind when he had never taken the trouble to put them there.

Another patient, a youth of nineteen, came to me at his parents' request. He had declined their offer of college or a year of travel, would give no thought to the future, saw no reason to change a single detail of a life in which every day was exactly like the day before—up at three in the afternoon, off to the neighborhood club to play the drums with a rock group, home and to bed at three in the morning.

He had a room under his parent's roof, a few dollars in pocket money from his father. He had a few T-shirts, two pairs of jeans, an outer garment of some sort. He even had a girl, who turned up at his wish whenever he thought hard enough about her. His mother gave him a teen-age meal, always the same—hamburger medium rare with ketchup, French fries, and a coke. If she offered him steak, roast chicken, Wiener schnitzel, he simply did not eat. He once went hungry for three days before she capitulated.

"What about ten years, five years from now?" I asked him.

"Five years from now will take care of itself. Only old people like you and my parents worry about the future," he told me. He had created a magic world of eternal youth in which he would never grow old, nothing would ever change, he need never do anything but what he was doing, day after day. "Wouldn't you like to live my life, Doctor?" he asked with engaging innocence. "I've got it made, man!"

As it happened, this boy's magic did not endanger his life, although it was a maimed life he was living. He smoked a little pot but he took no hard drugs. Other young people have gambled with their health, their sanity—and some have lost their lives—in this dangerous game of using magic tools to cope with difficult reality.

Family Magic, Business Magic

Magic creeps into every aspect of life, and older and presumably wiser men and women mistakenly use it to shape attitudes and make decisions. It can bring its misuser untold grief, to say nothing of the grief it may bring to others. A father founds a business, and as his son grows up he first hopes, then expects, then demands that the young man follow him into it and carry it on. "Why did I slave all these years to build up the business, if not for him?" he cries, forgetting that it was to satisfy his own need for achievement and success that he worked through the years.

How could he be so sure, all those years while his son was growing up, that the boy would go into his business? In the equation of magic, the world is a certainty and there are no exceptions, no mischances, only guarantees. The wish itself has power to bring about the wished-for event. The mere fact that a son had been born to him was assurance that his wish for a successor in his business was granted.

To many parents a child is not an individual but a magical projection of themselves, an object to be shaped for the life of their fantasy. What of the mother who brings up her daughter with an image of the kind of man she is to marry, a man who may have existed twenty or thirty years ago when the mother herself was young—or may never have existed at all outside of the mother's imagination? We see less of this than we did in a past generation, perhaps. Daughters today are somewhat more liberated from mothers' influence. But in almost everyone's acquaintance, in almost every family even, there have been maiden aunts, women who never married, not because they did not want to marry but because no young man who came to the house could match the mother's magical vision of a prospective son-in-law.

Mama and Papa magic has not altogether vanished. I

still have patients who come for help in making their escape from it. One young woman had been brought up on her mother's dream that she would become a prima ballerina and be enthroned in flowers, festooned with diamonds, and would climax her career, not with a Grand Duke, for even to this dreaming mother Grand Dukes were out of fashion, but at least with an oil millionaire for a husband. The girl worked hard at ballet school—what little girl could resist such a fairy tale future?—but her gifts were not enough even to keep her in the corps de ballet. And when she found herself selling behind a counter in Macy's to earn a living, she used good common sense, took secretarial training, and worked her way up to a reliable, decently paid private secretary's job. Along the way she came for help. She was confused and depressed—as who wouldn't be?— and the magic promise still haunted her. It was not easy to relinquish the dazzling dream and trim her sails to the unaccommodating winds of reality.

Her mother took it far harder. When the girl brought home her accountant husband-to-be, her mother greeted him with a stony face, and I am certain she never really believed her daughter could not have fulfilled her dream *if she had only tried hard enough!* Magic thinking is seductive, and when it fails, it puts out a thousand rationalizations—bad luck, world conditions, even the paranoiac explanation that "others" have interfered out of envy or ill will.

Magic-think even pervades the supposedly cool, realistic world of business. One young woman, who came to me for help through a postdivorce depression, seemed to be laboring under the belief that a corporation is a kind of benevolent organization. When her ex-husband stopped his payments of child support, she had gone to her superior and asked for a raise in salary to make up for the man's defection, and when it was refused she resigned in anger, to find herself not only without child support but with no income at all.

Another patient has become a floater, drifting from job to job. He is a conscientious worker who often puts in longer hours than are required on the job, but he suffers from the magical conviction that an employer should express appreciation of his worth without being asked, and should reward him with salary increases and promotions without being solicited. And so he quits job after job, with mounting resentment and paranoia, still seeking the oracular boss who will magically see and reward his unique abilities. But there is no such boss and no such magic. The cold reality is that management pays only as much as it must to keep its working force, that few if any individual employees are indispensable, and that exceptional abilities are sometimes rewarded but only in exceptional circumstances. Jobs, raises, and promotions are governed not by magic but by negotiation. The whole trade-union movement is based on this reality.

The Perils of Magic-Think

Among disturbed and unhappy people, magical belief is always present, and it is the function of serious therapy to focus on the misleading illusion, however deeply concealed. Often the patient's history explains the persistent magic compulsion, but rarely so dramatically as in the case of one very beautiful and sad young woman, who told me on her first visit that she wanted to die but did not know how to manage it.

Her magical belief, as it emerged, was that somewhere in the world she would find a replacement for her father, long dead but yet terribly vivid in her memory. He had been killed when she was four years old, while she, her family, and their neighbors, all Jews, were running away from the advancing Nazi army in Poland. They took refuge on a farm, and when German soldiers were stationed in the farmhouse, the courageous peasant woman hid them in a shed over the pigsty, where she fed them when she fed the pigs and shielded them from discovery for three long years.

In this terrible period the party could not wash, could not change their clothing, could speak only in whispers, and the child was kept from crying with a pillow over her mouth and always with the threat of being killed. She came to believe that she would be taken out and slaughtered in her turn like the pigs, and that her father

would save her if only he would come. She did not understand until much later that he had died.

Long after her escape with her mother, the nightmare memory haunted her with its menace of doom and its magical promise that her father would come and wipe out those hideous years. As a grown woman she was capable and self-supporting, dealing successfully with the real world—except in one respect. She still felt death hanging over her, and she still sought her father in all the older men she met in the course of business, many of whom mistook her childlike trust for sexual availability. The task of therapy was to set her free, not from the memory, which could never be expunged, but from its crippling aftermath, the magic compulsion to find a father, which made it impossible for her to find serenity in a normal life and normal relationships.

Magic makes people blind and deaf to reality. It guides them past it, finessing their escape from it in any way they can find, and the more gifted they are, the more convincing their rationalizations. They speak and hear their own justifications and they believe every word they say. Theirs is a special kind of disease, which I call mouth-and-ear disease.

That is why attention must be paid to their very individual sufferings, and why the entertaining instant therapies cannot ease their pain except momentarily. The touch-and-feel establishments are for the bored and the blasé and will do them no harm—and may even refresh them with a new kind of diversion. But as a haven for the deeply distressed, and for those who have been betrayed into folly and unhappiness by their own magic thinking, no diversionary measure can give them the strength and clarity they need to live with their existential realities.

In Praise of Magic

If we cannot take these exotic excursions seriously as therapies, do we then dismiss them? Not at all. With all their extravagances, the gurus have brought back something that was in truth missing from our assembly-line society. Knowingly or not, they are in tune with a natural force, an elemental human expression.

The magic therapies offer a weekend or a week of being free, creative, uninhibited, and unafraid, of releasing for a short run the demoniac desires and impulses that we all secretly believe—or at least hope—that we have within us. And by giving these jaunts the magical name of "therapy," we release our inner satyrs and demons in a safe context, without having to face the social consequences. We need our forays into magic, our Dionysian rites.

Magical thinking is a powerful force that wells up out of the deepest centers of our being. It is creative energy. It spurs imagination and fantasy, art and invention. It can bring comfort and serenity in the face of life-and-death situations, and it may even offer a life line to survival. Physicians recognize what they call the "will to live" in people rallying from grave illness or rehabilitating themselves from crippling disease or accident.

Imagine two men on a life raft, wallowing in a limitless ocean. One of them has already accepted the grim outcome of their situation. The other has grasped at the magical belief that, despite all probability, they will be rescued. Which of the two will still be alive when the rescuers come?

A French physician was once struck by the mysteriously high proportion of deaths among shipwrecked sailors and fishermen. He studied a large number of records gathered over many decades, and found that in most cases the men who perished had not suffered exposure, hunger, or thirst for fatally long periods, that they were not physically debilitated to the point of death. Some, indeed, were brought ashore still alive, only to die in the hospital. He could offer only psychological causes for their death—in effect, they died from loss of hope.

I find it more interesting to speculate on their shipmates who survived. What kept them alive? Can it have been a magical belief in their own powers of survival, in the value of life itself and of their own lives in particular? I imagine an unspoken, perhaps a wordless threnody sustaining these men—life is worth living, I am worth saving, I will be saved.

Magic or not, such a belief is what all therapies strive to instill, and it is beyond price.

But magic is a dangerous substitute for reality, unless we live in a Tibetan hamlet. In our world of complex relationships and continuous challenge, wishing does not make it so. And even if we escape actual harm, magic-think impoverishes our lives. It deprives us of the real experience of real people, in all their uniqueness and diversity, and it deprives us of our real selves. In a magic world, only the fantasizing part of the self can live—all the rest is lost. When we cut ourselves off from genuine interaction with others, we cut off the largest part of ourselves.

- *Don't confuse dreaming about life with living it.*

- *Your feelings by themselves are not a measure of reality.*

- *If you want more, ask for it; this applies in any relationship. Corollary: A corporation is not a benevolent institution.*

- *Living a fantasy life is fine until a real-life automobile knocks you down.*

- *Magical thinking is a powerful elixir but a dangerous medicine.*

Whither the
Pop Therapies?

3

We live in a regressed society, and one of the more
flamboyant signs of regression is the appearance of a
peculiar sexual elite. Its members are modish, sophisticated, and rebellious, and they see themselves as an advance guard of a social change that will strip us of our
sexual inhibitions and exorcise our Puritan prudery.
Their teaching tool for this liberating future is a spawn
of glossy magazines that are preoccupied with nudity,
male and female, with particular emphasis on the
graphic portrayal of genitalia, as if genitalia were the
total essence of human sexuality.

Far from being an avant-garde, this self-styled liberation movement is a step backward into infantilism. What it offers is the kind of titillations that commonly appeal to young adolescents barely out of puberty.

Many of this elite are sexual slummers. They will do anything for a quick trip that will not "involve" them. There is a hard core of advocates who defend unusual couplings, claiming that wife swapping and social sex have existed throughout man's history.

They should read a little of the history that they misquote so glibly. Rape, abduction, wife stealing have been accepted customs, yes—but not the institutionalized exchange of wives or the participation in sexual party games. Greek and Roman wives remained at the hearthside while their husbands reveled at stag banquets with prostitutes and concubines. When women who were not professional entertainers joined in open sexuality, it was invariably for religious or ritualistic purposes. Dionysius was not the editor of a slick sex rag. He was a god earnestly worshiped.

Sex slumming as it is practiced today cannot even be graded as licentious. Genuine licentiousness has often resulted in fine erotic art—the work of great painters and writers, the Greek and Roman poets, and the goliards of the high Middle Ages, those wandering scholars who kicked up their heels in northern Europe, making love and singing their lusty lyrics, many of which survive to this day in Carl Orff's *Carmina Burana.*

Unfortunately the goliards' verses are in low Latin, which precludes general enjoyment.

Are nudity and group sex really necessary to relieve us of sexual repression? Some of the encounter therapies have embraced this belief as a cornerstone principle. But to believe that everyone can be improved by lining up unclothed for the sexual equivalent of a square dance is to make quite an assumption about human sexuality.

I am reminded of a most attractive virgin of forty who came for consultation, not because she herself was troubled by her chastity but because it troubled her friends. Some of them, women as well as men, were so persistent in urging her to abandon her virginity that she had begun to wonder if indeed there was something wrong with her. Finally, in a spirit of open-mindedness that we might all emulate, she attended some of the intimacy marathons on the West Coast where nudity is part of the daily program.

In her first experience, mixed thermal bathing in the nude was optional, and perhaps because there was no pressure she enjoyed it. Then her fellow guests formed themselves into an "attack group," and acting in massed anarchy they assaulted her reticence and sense of privacy with relentless ferocity. It was as though, in a kind of collective unconscious, they had agreed that her virginity was the ideal, the ultimate target. She felt, she told me, that she had somehow strayed into a past century or another country, that she was being interrogated by a medieval inquisition for religious heresy or by the officers of a police state for political dissidence. She was helpless to defend herself against a group of sexual elitists who expressed at best a pitying contempt and at worst an aggressive, angry hostility for a woman who, in this day and age, still found celibacy a viable and happy alternative.

Her sessions with me revealed how harmonious a role her voluntary virginity played in her life. She conducted a small private day-care center, with just enough children for her to give her attention to each one. In her own home she was rearing a family of nephews and nieces whose mother had died and whose father had gratefully given them over to her care. She revealed not a trace of neurotic attachment to the children in her charge—it was an obvious possibility and I watched for signs, but found none. On the contrary, she combined a well-trained professionalism in child psychology with the empathy for children that makes a born mother or teacher. She was a woman of genuine warmth, humor, and sanity rare in our crazy world, and if we could have more forty-year-old virgins of her fiber we would all be the better for it.

Peak? Or Manic?

"Peak experience" is a term that recurs regularly in the encounter literature. It was originally coined by a psychologist of deep human sympathies who made it the centerpiece of a theory of individual growth that he called self-actualization. His name was Abraham Maslow, and few works of men have been bastardized so swiftly. He was adopted as the father of the encounter movement, but in actual fact he was in rebellion not so much against the traditional psychotherapies as against the behaviorists in the university departments of psychology who drew their picture of the human psyche from experiments with rats.

Maslow's message was a beautiful one and he himself was a beautiful person. I met him several times, and corresponded with him. He was a man in constant search—he vibrated with an intense belief in mankind's capacity to grow and transcend itself. He seemed obsessed with seeking opportunities for peak experiences, those distillations of a rare, elusive elixir that could fill the self to its ecstatic brim. I believe that in his restless search for a continuous state of ecstasy Maslow literally wore himself out and drove himself to an untimely death.

I have questioned some of Maslow's premises, wondering which of our many selves was to be actualized. The emotional self? The intellectual self? The instinctual self? The biological self?

The human being is a mass of complexities, but in one respect it is uniform. Both physiologically and psychologically it is geared to avoid destructive extremes. Every response has its counterresponse. When a healthy body experiences an outpouring of adrenalin in response to rage or fear, a countermechanism also goes into action that holds the pattern of glandular and nervous response within limits safe for the organism.

The senses all have their limits of responsiveness. The sense of smell is particularly quick to reach the fatigue level. A woman walks into the room wearing the most expensive scent, and your nose is delighted, but within minutes you can no longer smell it. The most beautiful music, too often played, becomes an annoyance; the most delightful raconteur, if he goes on too long, becomes a bore. And if such a thing were possible, imagine a continuous state of orgasm! The very thought is torture.

Society adds its own limits to our opportunities for peak experiences. We would find it inconvenient, at the least, to function ecstatically on our jobs, in our family relationships, in our dealings with bankers, grocers, plumbers, electricians, or while driving our cars or running our vacuum cleaners. To live at peak experience one has to be a poet in an attic, or a wealthy eccentric, or a hobo. And what is the distinction between living at peak experience and being manic?

Some of these questions preoccupied Maslow himself, and from his writings, one can glean that he was not wholly committed to peak experience as the alpha and omega of human life.

If Maslow had doubts, the encounterists did not. They embraced his assumptions and hugged them into shapes that he had not envisioned—as, for example, their place in a nude sensitivity-training course complete with warm swimming pool and excursions into crotchery.

Maslow suffered the misfortune of many creative thinkers, including even Freud to some extent, in that instead of students who would expand his ideas with further study and criticism, he was followed by a generation of apostles who grasped at the narrowest interpretation of his theory, gave it a simplistic form, and elevated it into a credo. Maslow's hope was to make relationships between people more honest and open throughout the whole spectrum of living, not just for a weekend marathon at fifty dollars a day plus air fare.

Of course, you can make your sex life or your emotional life the magnetic pole around which all your life revolves. But then you reduce your intellect to a servant engaged in rationalizing and justifying your emotions and your sex life. It is possible to build an entire philosophy, even a theology, on the theory of peak experience as a way of life. And in fact we have been seeing many people engaged in doing just that.

A psychological rebellion of some kind was due when Maslow arose with his inspired and eloquent teaching, and the pity is that his particular rebellion got stuck in the gimmicky rut of the touch-and-feel school. Yet, who can say that some of these rebellious therapies are not helpful, at least to a proportion of their followers? They remind me of the custom of "taking the waters" at a European spa that was so popular with the leisure class of a recent past.

In those days it was fashionable to complain not of the psyche but of the liver, although most of those people were not suffering from anything more than overeating and inactivity, with perhaps a touch of boredom. The evil-smelling baths and evil-tasting draughts, combined with diet, colonic irrigations, and therapeutic walks made them feel that they had paid their penance for their indulgences of the social season.

Some of the current therapies are also a kind of penance. Consider the "attack" groups against one member, often a newcomer, that seek to break down the defenses built up for twenty-five or thirty years of a lifetime. To be on the receiving end of such a session is surely as disagreeable as drinking sulphurous waters. Having one's genitals "eyeballed" may well make one feel like a penitent if not indeed a sacrificial victim! And, like the guests at the spas and the initiates of more ancient rites, the participants are all there voluntarily, they all make their votive offerings in cash or by credit card, and almost all of them emerge from a somewhat painful catharsis with a feeling of liberation, however short-lived.

Occasionally an esoteric therapy strikes a recognizably wholesome note. One charismatic guru held his therapeutic weekends at his northern California ranch house, set in the midst of his flourishing vineyards. He put his group to work from sunrise to moonrise, harvesting grapes, and when it was not grape harvest time he found other useful work for them to do, pruning, staking, setting out new shoots, or whatever. His followers were not naïve innocents. Everyone of them was intelligent and worldly enough to know that they were doing serf's work for their feudal host, and were paying him for the privilege.

And what of that? At the end of twelve hours of sweaty labor to which none of them was accustomed, with the added stimulus of wine and sex, they were ready and eager to believe that they had achieved "self-actualization" as promised. For people in normal health who spend their working days with telephones and typewriters and the jargon of their professions, physical labor outdoors is indeed a self-realization of a kind. And if it is productive work as well, work that "shows" in well-tended vines or baskets heaped with fruit, then it is also psychically gratifying.

Therapies of Conformity

Clearly the therapies of rebellion are striking against the constricted, overorganized lives most of us must live in a complex urban society that has squeezed out the beauty and blurred the sensibilities. But they are also aimed against the target of traditional psychotherapies.

The image of the psychoanalyst as an all-seeing, all-knowing divinity dealing out judgments in measured doses is, of course, a popular myth. But it is no myth that most psychoanalysts are conservative by temperament. Papa Freud was a humanizing radical in his time but in his personal life he was as square as any Kansas Kiwanian.

So it is not remarkable that many psychoanalysts have operated from their own conviction that their neurotic patients were unhappy because they were in conflict with society. From this it followed logically that a therapist's task was to smooth out the rough edges and help his patient slip easily into the general orthodoxy, to find peace through conformity. As one analyst said, not altogether in jest, "What can I do for a suburban housewife except help her to feel happier while she plays bridge all afternoon?"

Fashions in conformity are not uniform. In Europe we have had Catholic analysts and Marxist analysts. Recently I heard a patient complain of his Jewish analyst who berated him because, although he traveled abroad every year, he had never gone to Israel. "How is it possible that you are a Jew and you never go to Israel?" the analyst demanded, with a vigor that betrayed his own preference in conformity. The patient went away unconformed, still determined to make his own travel plans.

One of the thrusts against conformist therapy has come from homosexuals. For years the medical profession labeled homosexuality a sickness and homosexuals went into therapy to be "cured," that is, to be rendered heterosexual. The therapy recorded a striking lack of success. No matter how convincingly the analysts probed into recollections of a mother's seductiveness or a father's failure to provide a proper male image, most of their patients resisted the cure.

In time many of them rebelled outright, insisting that the trouble was not in themselves but in a society that refused to accept their unorthodox form of sexuality and drove them into neurosis by its pressures. Today we see homosexuals living happily—or at least so they say—in their own choice of relationships, no more neurotic than anyone else.

Another attack came from the women's liberationists, who branded Freud the original male chauvinist. Freud confessed more than once that women were an unfathomable mystery, but he did not for that reason refrain from trying to fathom them. And a good case can be made against many of his followers, with the exception of Karen Horney who observed that what was wrong with women was mostly the effect of society, not of their biology.

Women have been, if not more neurotic than men, at least more willing to seek help. I think of one woman who was in no respect a women's liberationist. She had no ambitions for a career as an artist, although she was gifted, but she managed to create a highly artistic environment for her husband throughout a long and singularly happy marriage. When her husband died, frightened at the prospect of being alone for the first time since her marriage at eighteen, she went to an analyst for help. Her analyst happened to be an orthodox Freudian, and when she left him after a few sessions she said to a friend, "I know I'm screwed up, but one thing I know is not wrong with me is penis envy."

Screaming It Out

Most of us abhor our ignorance of what the future has in store for us. We recoil from the uneasy feeling that we are not in control of our destiny. We find the uncertainties of life hard to accept; they cause us anxiety if not downright depression. And therefore many people try to shake off their uncertainties by resorting to magical devices that give them the illusion of control. They toy and tinker with various occult practices —astrology, palmistry, tarot cards, I-Ching, or whatever happens to be the going fashion. Secretly or overtly, they are trying to open doors to the future, to see into the distance with myopic eyes. They have not developed a philosophy for living in the present.

Not surprisingly, the reverse is also true. We can be spooked by the past, made anxious or distressed by some remembered injustice or unfulfilled need of childhood. Many people therefore seek a scream therapist who shows them how to regress into childhood where the injury occurred. This is accomplished by a systematic regime of breaking down the adult intellectual and rational approach to living and encouraging the patient to scream out his rage and frustration like a child in a tantrum, thus presumably ventilating the blocked passages where the fantasies of hurt and deprivation have been lodged.

Therapeutic regression is not a new idea. Up to a few years ago the technique of hypnotherapy was fashionable, and patients were regressed by hypnosis to resurrect their real or fantasied experiences of childhood. Freud and his orthodox followers relied heavily on the recapture of childhood memories, and a whole generation grew up on the facile interpretation of Freudian theory that they were not responsible for their adult personalities, that they were the result of what their parents did to them, or failed to do. Side by side with this assumption of parental guilt was another, equally fanciful assumption, that parents existed to make children happy.

This is an astonishing piece of nonsense that, with one brief exception, was never true throughout the course of human history. Parents have loved their children, have cared for them more or less tenderly at all times and in all societies, but they have not devoted themselves to their children's happiness. The upper classes, relegated their children to wet-nurses, nannies, governesses, boarding schools. The working classes put them out as apprentices. And the very poor sent them out to beg and steal, sold them into slavery and prostitution, did whatever they had to do for sheer survival.

The one exception was a period in recent American history, between the first and second world wars, when mothers and fathers studied how to make their children happy, made sacrifices to give them whatever they wanted, felt guilty over every mistake they made in feeding, weaning, or toilet training, and were actually afraid to impose discipline or punishment. It was an extraordinary interlude in the long history of parent-child relationships, and European visitors observed in amazement what was called the child-centered society. The consequences are still being felt, in a generation that continues to look for the source of its miseries in its parents' sins whether of commission or omission.

I talked to one of these patients who had gone into scream therapy to exorcise her parents' failures. She reeled off a long list of complaints against them, until finally I asked her, "And what are you doing? You have no children, you are not even getting married. Aren't you going to show us all what a good parent can be?"

"Oh, no!" she exclaimed, physically recoiling from the suggestion. "I'd never want to live the life my mother had!"

So it seems that some of this complaining generation decline to become parents at all, and others have no intention of putting themselves out for their children. Self-sacrificing parents are a dwindling minority. Parents today more and more expect their children to stand on their own feet, just as they expect someone other than themselves—the government perhaps—to look after their aging parents.

So scream therapy may well be on the way to oblivion, if only because the targets will have vanished. One can imagine that a scream session in the not too distant future might go this way:

Therapist. Your mother didn't come running, did she, when you wet your pants? She didn't drop what she was doing and rush upstairs as you stood shivering and leaking, to kiss and comfort you?

Regressed patient. No! the mean old witch! [Screaming.] I hate you! I hate you!

Therapist. And she forgot one day that there would be nobody to meet the school bus when you came from kindergarten, and you had to walk all the way up the long driveway to your house alone and frightened. She shouldn't have forgotten, should she?

Regressed patient. You horrid old meanie, you, shouldn't have forgotten! [Scream, scream].

Therapist. And your mother and father left you in summer camp while they traveled all over Europe in a Mercedes-Benz, and you couldn't sit in your mother's lap while she ate her dinner every night?

Regressed patient. You went off and left me—you went off to enjoy yourself while I was so miserable—and just for that I'm going to kill you both [scream, scream] with my [scream scream] silver spoon!

Whether or not parents will have to be invented to be raged against, we cannot foretell. But scream therapy patients have told me that there is cathartic uplift after a bout of screaming, and this alone may be worth the price of admission.

The Man Who Couldn't Stop

The feeling of relief and exuberance after a session of group screaming has been testified to by many patients I have treated. They have also reported a strange phenomenon of group paranoia directed against such generalized targets as social injustice, the federal government, "the system," and even—depending on their orientation—against welfare recipients. Bitching about their parents led them inevitably, it seemed, to bitching about country, corporations, prices, taxes, the young, the old, the squares, the hip. When they ran out of personal grievances to scream about, other grievances rushed in to fill the vacuum, grievances against a world that refused to give them the large share of its goodies, to which they felt themselves entitled as a matter of right. They took to acting out the character in the cartoon who sent searing letters to his local newspaper every Wednesday and Saturday, signing himself "Outraged Citizen."

But one of the graduates of scream therapy came to me in genuine distress. His was an extreme case: He could not stop screaming. He had had 120 hours of

Freudian analysis beforehand, but his feelings of detachment and alienation had not abated, and so on his therapist's advice he had enrolled in a scream therapy group. He completed the course, but with a screaming hangover.

He told me how at his first session he had been confronted with an attack group who systematically worked to break down his controls. They urged him on, not only to scream but to use physical violence—pushing, wrestling, arm-wrenching methods of settling an argument that he had been glad to abandon at the age of ten for the more civilized, or at least less painful, processes of reasoning and negotiation. The group ridiculed his restraint and persuaded him to demonstrate his contempt for the intellectual process by urinating in his pants, which he did.

The trouble with the therapy for him was that it was too successful. He screamed at his wife, his children, his neighbors, and finally at his boss. His home life collapsed, he lost his job, and he became paranoidally defensive and assaultive. All the rational controls that he had built up through thirty of his thirty-five years had been shattered, and all he had left were feelings of rage. It took a long time to woo back his intellectual faculty, to separate him from his instant rages and eventually to accomplish a separation of his feelings from his being.

Living by one's emotions contains a multitude of

dangers. Even in societies that, compared with ours, are relatively primitive, the individual is surrounded by rules and restraints, and a Robinson Crusoe living alone on a desert island would risk his life if he functioned by tantrum rather than reason. Feelings are a rich part of our humanity, but they are not the whole self; and when they are unguided by the rational mind and left to run rampant, they can destroy everything of value in an individual's life.

But the real harm that our uncontrolled emotions can do is in cutting us off from the relationships that sustain us, challenge us, keep us alive and human. I am not speaking now of spontaneous expressions of love, longing, delight—or their opposites—that enliven or at least clarify our own and the other's life together. A strong feeling, even of anger or resentment, is far better aired than buried to fester, as we all know.

On the other hand, spouse, children, colleagues, friends can scarcely be expected to hold still under an incessant barrage of high-voltage emotion, whether of enthusiasm or revulsion. Sooner or later they will run for cover. We have all known people with whom we could be friends, if only they did not wear us out with the unvarying intensity of their feelings, or their expression of feelings. If only they would discharge some of that intensity in writing poetry or painting pictures, and come to us with a little more composure!

One such woman of my acquaintance is bearable for

about five minutes. Her husband, although a dry-as-dust pedantic, is a relief, and I have no doubt that his suppression of all spontaneity is a survival mechanism for living with his volcanic wife. I have often wished that I could pick up this woman, as I would do with an overexcited child, and carry her off to remain alone in a quiet room where she could cool down enough for human communication.

When we teach our children, preferably by example, a reasonable control of their emotions, in my judgment we are not repressing them and certainly not crippling their self-expression. On the contrary, we are giving them a mode of expression that is essential to their future life among people, one to which others can listen and respond.

- *Virginity is not a disease, and sexual selectivity is not an infirmity.*

- *The rational mind is a survival tool for living.*

- *We can be overdosed by our senses, too, just like drugs.*

- *What is the difference between living at peak experience and being manic?*

- *Scream if you must, but remember—someone may scream back at you.*

- *Psychotherapists who still play God had better have their heads re-examined.*

- *Of women's troubles, penis-envy is the least.*

- *Your life is your own when you stop complaining about what your parents did to you.*

Hotlines to Nowhere

II

Me, Myself, and I

4

They are a new breed of people. You would not see them as strange or eccentric, and what you might hear in ordinary conversation with one of them would not cause you so much as a raised eyebrow. They are affable, bright, often charming. But if the dynamics of their beliefs and behavior were laid open, it would scare the daylights out of anyone who values the humanity of human beings.

Many of them staff the giant electronic-computer, multimedia, multinational corporations, but they can be found anywhere, and everywhere—in professions, on university faculties, in the younger management echelons of business at home and abroad. They are a subspecies of the educated and moderately affluent middle class, and their normal habitat is urban. They are the neo-Orwellians, the hyperindividualists, and the theology they live by is crowned by a trinity: Me, Myself, and I.

They stretch across two generations, and some are married, some are parents, but they are committed neither to marriage nor to parenthood, nor even to friendship. They have closed the door on all that as a delusion of the past, and they float in an erratic orbit of newly found freedom.

Some of them come to see me, but not to find a way out of a tangled emotional underbrush or to have a scrambled inner world reordered. They come to find endorsement of their chosen rationale, to have their belief system blessed and reinforced, not by me, because I will not give my blessing, but by others like themselves who may have drifted into my groups.

I think of a woman, the mother of four children aged ten to sixteen, who came to tell me about her husband, a psychiatrist of forty-three. Without warning one day, he had hurled a bombshell at her.

"There must be something more to life than this," he told her. "I'm leaving."

And leave he did. He walked out of the family scene, went to Africa, and after a time his child support payments ceased. His wife and four children moved to modest quarters in a suburb. When the money ran out, she took a job. Then one day she also quit. She quit her job, her home, her children, and went to Hawaii to live.

Before she went she told me her decision. "I'll be damned if I'll spend my life working for his bastards. He's right. There's more to life and I'm going to get my share. I've got some good years left. Let the state take care of the kids."

Her children had become his bastards. But, as she said, the state could take care of them, and it did.

Another woman, in her twenties, has a child of three. She finds no pleasure in bringing up her child; to her it is an unmitigated bore. Her husband feels no differently, and from the time the child was born, he bitterly resented the expense of a baby-sitter for their evenings out. So she took to going out alone. She went to bars, not so much to drink as to flirt and pick up men.

Why did they have a child at all? The response was startling. They wanted the spice of danger, the risk of seeing whether or not she would conceive without benefit of the pill or a diaphragm. So they played Russian roulette in bed. If they lost, she said, then she would at least enjoy the novelty of motherhood. They lost.

By the time the child was three, the novelty had worn off. The wife tried manipulating her mother into taking over the care of the child, but her mother declined; she, too, wanted to be free to live her own life. She tried various neighborhood child-care pools. Finally, the pair agreed to put the child out for adoption, and not long afterward they also parted from each other.

Gone Are the Gods

These people sound like monsters but they are not monsters. They are an end result of social change, change that has come at breakneck speed over the past two decades. Theirs is a response to the loss of a central belief, something that people have needed throughout history. With nothing left to cling to, they have fashioned as the core of the selfhood a theology of the self, with no bonds, no restraints. From the clinical point of view, they are sociopaths, people who accept no role in society and no responsibility to anyone or for anyone but themselves.

It has happened before in history that the core of man's being has been chipped away by great events. In ancient times, virtue, valor, and the mythology of the gods gave life its meaning. Then, in the Western world, came the supportive faiths of Judaism, Christianity, Islam. In all of them, man was the lord of a God-created universe.

Galileo's shocking discovery that man's domain, the earth, was not the center of the universe jarred these belief systems. With Darwin came another shock, the evidence that we were neither gods nor angels but cousins to the apes. Marx shook our faith in the state, in government, in the economic system by which we earned our living. Freud jolted us by his revelation that our reason did not guide our behavior, that we were toys at the whim of unconscious motivations.

Two world wars, the atomic bomb, the Vietnam War, the desperate flight of whole populations from place to place, and assassinations, terrorist bombs, the full horrors of man's inhumanity to man—this century has lived through it all, has actually witnessed much of it with eyes and ears on the little magic screen in our own homes. All this we know, but it is worth recapitulating as we trace the effects on the human psyche.

Perhaps the fragile faiths to which we still clung could have survived, but something else was meanwhile being destroyed. Our last refuge, the family, was being shattered. Man's most ancient divinity, older than the Olympian gods, older than Yahveh, Allah, or the Christian Trinity—the Mother Goddess—was toppling.

The industrialized, urbanized, technologized Western world had already shaken her altar, and the pill and women's liberation—both equally consequences of the scientific and technological revolutions—completed her fall. With the Mother Goddess, keeper of the children and the hearth, the last security blanket was gone.

What we are seeing is disillusion with everything and everyone except one's own individual self. The new people, the hyperindividualists, are the people of the post-hippie world.

The hippies themselves still had faith. They slammed the door on their own families, or what remained of them, and went forth into the wilderness to form their pseudofamilies, the communes. They tried naïvely, often ineptly, to shake themselves free of the society they saw as inhuman and antihuman, and create a mini-world of their own. They were a minority but their ideas spread to people who did not drop out, people both older and younger, who still tried to make it within the society that they, too, felt had lost its humanity.

But the hippies found that they still needed help from the families they despised or the government they hated, in the form of cash or welfare checks. The communes fell apart, and their members drifted back into cities and towns. Many of them still live on the edge of economic survival, a shabby intellectual proletariat without even the charm of the old-time hobo.

Feed, Fornicate, and Flee

In five short years the hippie culture transformed all youth, and it magnetized the older generation and those on the threshold of adulthood. It dramatized the loss of faith in society and its institutions, the contempt for the past, and the hopelessness of the future. Its here-and-now philosophy and its working-class fashions were exported throughout the Western world.

Its fashions still survive; the more ragged and bleached the jeans, the more outrageous their price tag. The work clothes the hippies affected are no longer even worn by workmen who drive to the job in their cars. A woman told me of trying to buy a birthday present for her son-in-law, a brilliant university mathematician, who would use only bandanna handkerchiefs of the coarsest cotton to blow his highly educated nose. She found some—at $3.50 each. Even Woolworth's had only white handkerchiefs.

When the hippie movement collapsed, it seems that the last vestige of human relationships collapsed with it. The new people care for no one but themselves. They come in two life styles, and the first of the two are the hedonists, the pleasure seekers.

There must be more to life, say these people, and they look for it in their pleasures. They have no goal except to enjoy themselves, to please their appetites and their senses. "What else is there?" some of them have asked me, but they smile at the answers I offer them. They are willing to use and misuse their bodies, to wear themselves out before their time.

I find clues in their background. The human child learns about relationships in the family, and for these people the family had already disintegrated. I am not speaking of divorce. Divorce can be wholesome. I am speaking of the coldness of families that still continue, at least in outward form.

One of them, an educated, intelligent man in his forties, told me about his mother. She is an interesting, vital, attractive woman, but his chief memory of his childhood was the resentment with which she served a meal. She made no secret of it—she hated housework, hated cooking, could not wait until her son, her only child, grew up and got out of the house.

And in fact he no sooner entered college than his parents moved to a more elegant, more expensive apartment. But it was also much smaller, so that there was no room for the boy. All his boyhood possessions, his teen-age books and recordings and scrapbooks of sports heroes, the high school banners and photographs—the "kid trash," as his mother smilingly called it—disappeared, and when he came home for vacations, he slept like a transient guest on the living-room sofa. His visits were "cool." His parents, immersed in their social and professional lives, made the concession of taking him out to dinner once or twice during his holidays, but for the rest of the time he was on his own.

No matter—that was the way it had been throughout his high school years, and he was used to it. He was a nice kid and he had no trouble cadging meals at the homes of his friends. The college years were the same —he had perfected the art of making himself a guest. Now, as an adult, he finds himself always on the hunt for young women who will give him dinner in their one-room studio apartments and, for dessert, serve him with sex.

He tells me, "But I want a wife, I want some permanence, I want to get married!" I have heard this threnody now for some ten years. He will never make a permanent relationship, will never marry unless at some future time he and one of the many women who share his kind of life settle down together out of sheer fatigue.

In every urban center, there are thousands of such young, lonely women, ready and willing to provide these dual services, and thousands of young, lonely males who take it as their right to feed, fornicate, and flee. They feel no obligation, not even of simple civility. They may sometimes bring a bottle of wine, or some sticks of marijuana, for their own pleasure and only incidentally the girl's. But it would never occur to one of these young men to bring flowers, or a small personal gift of something she might like for herself. That would imply some feeling for her as another human being, and feeling is for squares.

Rabelais wrote of the Abbaye de Thélème, the Convent of Pleasure, where the only monastic rule was *Fais ce que vouldras,* "Do as thou wilt." But his monks and nuns contented themselves with the pleasures of lordly folk that were forbidden to the clergy and denied to the poor. They had sumptuous rooms, handsome apparel, fountains, flowers, jewels, perfumes, and the leisure to sing, dance, go riding, go hawking, and dine to satiety on rich foods. The Sybarites in their Greek colony in Italy did the same, lolling on rose-petaled couches and zoning their city so that the sounds and smells of working folk would not disturb them.

But nowhere in recorded history have I read of such cold-hearted, manipulative, joyless hedonism as these pleasure seekers of the late-twentieth century now pursue.

"Look to Your Own Two Hands"

The second life style of hyperindividualism is even more frigid and more joyless. It follows the teaching of an old adage: "If you need help, look to your own two hands."

The maxim merely recommends self-reliance, an old-fashioned, durable virtue. But these people look to their own hands with a vengeance. They ask no help and give none. They form no ties. They have no friends, only colleagues at work and passing acquaintances who share their leisure. They are often enormously competent and often fiercely ambitious, and they earn well, live well, take very good care of themselves. They join athletic clubs, play tennis or squash the year round, go skiing, drive expensive sports cars, go sailing in their own boats.

They are the pets of the multinational corporations,

because they willingly pick up at a moment's notice and fly to a new assignment halfway around the world. They have no emotional ties, no relationships that are not readily replaceable wherever they find themselves. Their security is in themselves, and in the impersonal tribal father, the corporation, that moves them around the country and the world as needed, gives them promotions and salary raises on schedule, pays their medical bills if they are sick, and will retire them with a comfortable pension at the age of sixty-five if they manage to live that long.

There are thousands of young men—and there will soon be large numbers of young women—who come out of the universities each year with a graduate degree in science, mathematics, one of the technological specialties, or business management, and go straight onto the bottom rung of the ladder at IBM or ITT or General Electric or General Dynamics. On the day they take the job, their entire future is laid out for them. Salaries, promotions, pension fund, medical insurance, life insurance—all are neatly data-processed from the beginning to the end of their working lives. Big Daddy will look after them, and unless Big Daddy himself—in other words, the whole corporate world—collapses, they are safe within their cool, encapsulated selves.

Other hyperindividualists are more adventurous. They scorn the tidy life plan the corporate Big Daddies offer them, and go into the less secure but more exciting world of finance, advertising, the cabalistic mysteries called "research and development," the grant-supported science laboratories of the now skyscrapered groves of academe, or just business.

Or they circulate, going from one to another, with sabbaticals for pleasure and adventure in between. A young woman told me how she had spent some months with one such adventurer who had cut loose from one orbit and was not yet ready to enter another. He was a man just turned forty, of splendid physique, who might have been a professional athlete, but he had other, more intellectual gifts as well. He was a businessman who had inherited a small electronics firm from his father, built it into a bigger one, sold it for a sizable capital gain, and promptly left his wife and teen-age children to live his own free-style life. He exchanged his small sailboat for a larger, sea-going vessel, took our young woman aboard as cook, crew, and sexual companion, and set sail for tropical waters.

After six months the girl was back. She had loved the boat, loved the life, enjoyed every minute of sun and sea and freedom from reality. Why, then, had she left this carefree life to come back to the grimy real world? She confessed: She could no longer stand living with this man.

This handsome, witty, sophisticated man had turned her utterly cold. She said, "He never seemed to see me as a person, a human being. I was just there, a warm body—to cook, to help sail the boat, to swim with, drink with, eat with, have sex with, but never to communicate with, to share real feelings with. I felt frozen out. I came back to this chilly city to get warm!"

The surprising fact here is that she was something of a free-floating hyperindividualist herself, one who had never formed a lasting attachment. But she acknowledged that in that romantic setting of tropical airs and palm-fringed islands she had begun to feel unfamiliar stirrings. The man, too, had been warm, affectionate; they had had a honeymoon at the beginning. She thought she was in love, and began to dream of a life with this man.

But the moment she began to show her real feelings, to bare her real self, he turned cool. Sometimes she cried, sometimes she stormed, and at those times he simply showed her his back. If they were at sea, he bent over his navigating charts. If they were in port, he took the dinghy and went ashore.

She said, "It was a shame, because we had so much going for us. We laughed at the same jokes, played the same games, had the same view of life—that it was something to be lived, not moped over. We were great in bed together, at least until I began to feel the chill.

"But I was not a woman, not a person, to him. I was there just to serve his needs but God forbid I should have needs of my own. I was never there as myself, only as another tool for his convenience and his enjoyment. Do you know, he treated me the same way he treated his boat. He took good care of us both, managed us both with great skill. He took pride and pleasure in me just the way he did in his boat—as long as I was obedient to the helm. . . ."

And there she had put her finger on it. As long as she was obedient, as long as she served her function.

The Functionalists

For the hyperindividualist has no use for other people as people, only as functions. The hyperindividualist uses people the way men use machines, and the way they have traditionally used prostitutes. A man may talk to the prostitute, may tell her his troubles with his business, with his wife. He may even ask her about her own life, but that is not out of feeling, only out of curiosity. She is nothing more than a sexual service station and he pays for the service just as he pays the garage mechanic who services his car.

Using other human beings as functions is commonplace in business, but even there it was not always so. In the old-fashioned family business the boss knew all his employees, knew their home situations, their personal peculiarities—this one was quick-tempered but loyal, that one was slow but reliable. He may have treated them well or ill, but he knew them as people. In modern business, people are no longer people. They are employees, or competitors, or customers, or creditors. A man's secretary is his secretary, and if, as we are told, he may also have sex with her during the noon hour, then she is simply serving an additional function for him besides keeping his appointment book and taking his dictation.

In the old days even a servant was not a function. We have only to see a Molière comedy or a Mozart opera, or reruns of the popular television series about the Edwardian household, *Upstairs Downstairs*, to be reminded that the gentleman's valet and the lady's maid were very much persons in their own right.

Today there are husbands who make functions of their wives and wives who make functions of their husbands, and children and parents who make functions of each other. A son serves his function for his father by carrying on the father's business, or by doing his father credit as a successful professional man. A daughter may do the same by making a creditable marriage or, as women achieve more equal opportunities, by carrying on the business or achieving a fine professional career.

The hyperindividualist does not always get his way. Like the young woman on the yachting adventure, people are not always willing to behave as functions. But, for the hyperindividualist, this is no disaster. People who merely serve as functions are as interchangeable as automobile parts.

I have in mind a medical man, an able and successful surgeon in his forties, who had a charming, spirited young wife. He was a prima donna among hyperindividualists, and she waited on him hand and foot. But she was too spirited and independent to be nothing more to him than a willing handmaiden, and when she rebelled he turned all the force of his forceful personality against her. He gave her such a psychological beating before he consented to a divorce that it took a long course of therapy to restore her battered selfhood.

He paid no price, neither of remorse nor of guilt. He simply found himself another wife. The second wife was a successful business woman in her own right. She was also older than he by quite a margin, and she was so strikingly plain that she had long since given up all hope of winning a husband.

Then came this handsome, distinguished surgeon, like a knight on a white horse, to rescue her from her spinsterhood. She gave up her business, gave up her independence, and joyfully went into bondage. At last report she still waits on him, pampers him, flatters him, keeps his house, entertains his guests, presumably gives him sex whenever he wants it, and is still so grateful to him for marrying her that she not only does not mind being treated as a function, she laps it up as a kitten laps up cream.

So, you see, it all depends. But a curious sidelight is that apparently the hyperindividualist is not as invulnerable to all feeling as he—and we—may believe. There is a chink in his self-centered armor. This man has never forgiven his first wife for rebelling against him. Even more significant, he has not forgiven the

psychiatrist who bound up his wife's psychological
wounds after he had thrown her out, and helped her
to walk upright again in her own person.

The Fear of Feeling

Hanging over the hyperindividualist like a polluting
cloud is the fear of experiencing deep feeling. Emotional frigidity is a prevailing symptom of our times.
To experience life coolly, to shut away deep feelings,
let alone passions, may be a defense against an era
of violence and inhumanity, but it also tends to shut
out compassion.

Many of the characters in Harold Pinter's plays are
archetypes of passionlessness, people who reach out to
others in a vain attempt to light a flame of communica-
tive feeling. In the arts, romantic feelings have long
ago been declared dead. Their place has been taken
by abstractions in music, painting, sculpture, ballet.
Nonobjective art, the passionless ballets of Balanchine
and Robbins—these are accurate reflections of a period
in history when open and free-flowing emotion is in-
admissible and only a geometrically orderly state of
mind is tolerable. Call it the emotional ice age.

The flight from feeling has more commercial evidence. The fashion in greeting cards is to avoid warmth
and sentiment, whether the occasion is a celebration or
a crisis. "Get well" cards to send to sick friends read

more like "Drop dead." One example spells out the theme of them all. On its face it says, "It could be worse . . ." and on the inside it continues, ". . . it could be ME!"

The decor of hotels and homes has turned pale with neutral beige shades. Where are the twentieth-century equivalents of the hospitable turkey-red carpet, the rosy bedroom furnishings? Shades of red that induce warm, affectionate feelings have all but disappeared from public and domestic environments, as we notice when we go abroad and find ourselves in the welcoming red and gold glow of an old-fashioned hotel, or a jewel of a theater that has not yet suffered redecoration in the chilly modern taste.

Gone also are the boudoir chair and the chaise longue, invitations to sexual courtship. Instead, people have cool sex in a setting of chromium, glass, and steel, an indoor echo of the apartment building's sterile geometric architecture. The antihero in novels is not new, but now we have a growing epidemic of non-achievers, sufferers, and impotent males in the grip of anomie, the social and psychological emptiness that is the end result of hyperindividualism.

Certain social scientists, even theologians, view the growth of the Me, Myself, and I trinity as the inevitable wave of the future. They gleefully predict what the year 2000 will bring in revolutionary new forms of human coupling. Embryo transplants and frozen-sperm implants will bring human procreation in line with modern technology, while sex itself will be served by group marriages, revolving sexual triangles, and that current favorite, the co-marital relationship in which two wives share one husband, or a "satellite" partner, usually female, joins the monogamous pair on occasion; she is a kind of "extra" who waits offstage until she is summoned to add an extra fillip to the action on the matrimonial couch.

Might not some of these interdisciplinary energies be better expended on stabilizing the simple one-to-one relationship? There are still unplumbed mysteries in the human personality, quite enough of them to keep all those trained minds and research moneys at work. Would we not like to learn why two intelligent fools lose sight of each other's precious uniqueness and break up their relationship after a promising beginning, rather than spend our creative powers inventing new ways to avoid relationships altogether?

Americans were the first in Western society to develop the mechanics of quickie or matinée sex during lunch hours, between planes, interspersed with business engagements and conference discussions. We have now exported the "rabbit nibble," as someone has aptly described it, to the very home of *amour* where courtship, foreplay, and all the refinements of lovemaking have been traditional. We hear that the long, leisurely luncheon and afternoon with a mistress, once sacred to French businessmen, is declining, that the very institution of the mistress in France is dying. Like the hamburger and fast-food counters that are replacing the little inexpensive, family-run restaurants, the American way of snack-sex is taking over. And all this is in the service of sex as a function, without feeling.

In India a man may watch his wife drown in the river and make no effort to rescue her. He will grieve, but he will accept her death in the calm belief that it was her preordained fate to die by drowning. The devout of many faiths accept the suffering and death of a loved one as the will of God, but this does not mean that they have no feeling.

An anthropologist recently described a mountain people in Africa, the Iks, who as a matter of course take scraps of food from their children. These are people who have lost their ecological base and are in fact starving. Still, they seem to us demented. We know many stories of starving parents who give whatever food they can lay hands on to their children, even though they themselves may be dying. In the desperate first winter of the Pilgrim colony at Plymouth, the greatest number of fatalities were those of mothers. They had gone without food themselves, giving their meager rations to their children.

Here in the affluent Western world we do not have a fatalist religion, nor do we live on the edge of survival. Yet, we read of people safe within the four walls of their apartment, who will not put out a hand to the telephone and call the police, while they listen to a murder victim's cries for help coming in at their windows. Reading these stories, we are shocked, and reporters go to those people and ask them why. But we do not need to ask, because we know the answer.

People do not want to become involved in another's fate. They have put away compassion, have put away feelings. They are all, to a greater or lesser degree, hyperindividualists, shut into their own little apartments, their own little selves.

Yet They Weep at Movies

But I have observed a curious fact about hyperindividualists I have known. They weep at plays and movies, and even music that evokes emotion can stir them to tears. Many of us do this, but for people of the emotional ice age it is surely out of character!

It is no mystery, not even a contradiction. It is simply an unspoken confession that hyperindividualism is not enough, that the religion of Me, Myself, and I does not satisfy their deeply human needs. Because however coolly, however rationally the hyperindividualist may deny his need for fellow feelings, for relationships of affection and interdependence, the need is there. It is part of our human heritage.

Man has been a social animal from his birth. So are our evolutionary cousins, the apes, and our more distant relatives, the monkeys. This is as true as the much-advertised "territorial imperative" and the aggressiveness of the "killer ape" that is presumed to be our direct evolutionary ancestor. The very name "killer ape" is a libelous misnomer. It implies that he killed wantonly, but all we know of him is that he was not a vegetarian like the surviving apes but a meat eater, a hunter who killed for his food. All apes, and presumably the meat-eating ape as well, have lived in family groups. So did the first humanoids, and the cave dwellers of the Ice Age, and the family and kinship and tribal groups that eventually peopled the earth.

We have laughed at the grotesque Neanderthal man, our Stone Age forebear with his too-long arms and too-short legs, his face with too little forehead and too much jaw. But the Neanderthal people of the geological Ice Age were more human than some of our emotional ice age people are today. They were kinder to their aged, at least when the harsh conditions of their life allowed. As the archaeologists read the evidence of one cave, members of the family chewed the tough food for their arthritic, toothless old parent of perhaps forty-five. They buried their dead with loving care, and in one grave that has been excavated, they laid the body of a young man prematurely dead on a bed of pine boughs and hundreds of wildflowers that they had toilsomely gathered from the hillsides. I can tell you the names of the wildflowers, too, if you doubt this, because the paleobotanists have identified them for us.

Yes, you say, but in those days people needed each other to survive. True, just as they needed the aggressive killer instinct to survive. Both are built into the human psyche, and who is to say which can be dispensed with today? The aggressive instinct can be channeled, and must be channeled, into productive pathways because we can no longer afford war. But what urgency is there to deny our need for communicating, for caring, for sharing? And into what pathways might it be channeled that would serve us better?

The hyperindividualists have a hotline to nowhere, because people need each other even more today than did Neanderthal men in the Ice Age. People need people to speak to them, to care about them, to cast off roles and pretensions and reveal their naked, vulnerable selves to each other. Now, more than ever before in the world, we need each other to lighten the terrible burden of existential loneliness.

- *As a way of life, hedonism is like a forest fire that burns to the edge of the sea—it has no future.*

- *It is not enough merely to respect another's uniqueness—we must defend it, even against ourselves.*

- *When we use our relatives and friends as functions, we dehumanize them and ourselves as well.*

- *The fringe benefits of the corporate life don't include insurance against the disease of hyperindividualism.*

- *The flight from feeling is also a form of pollution— it pollutes the human atmosphere.*

- *If we choose to live in an emotional ice age, can we keep from freezing to death?*

Out of This World

5

For some time there has been an energetic movement, called the Consciousness Revolution, to explore what are claimed to be the frontiers of the mind, to expand the limits of consciousness, and to experiment with a bizarre assortment of supernatural phenomena.

As I perceive this trend, we are in the grip of a national lightheadedness, brought on partially by our success in outer space and partially by the need to fill the vacuum left by our eroded belief systems. The loss of beliefs is fundamental; and I hold it as an axiom that without religious, philosophic, or intellectual ballast, man bobbles through life like a cork.

What is the rationale of these venturers into the far-out realms of Supermind, Superconscious, Supernatural? For they do have a rationale. Since the world is in chaos and the human species is going down the drain in any case, they seem to say, then let us escape to more rarefied levels and blot out the horrors. Let us call upon deep and ancient mysteries, repackaged for modern consumers, to solace us in our personal disasters and our loneliness. Let us climb upstairs to new floors of the mind and shut the doors on the whole bloody mess downstairs.

Instead of trying to form connections with earthly realities, let us float right out of this world and make new links by way of an altered consciousness. Let us talk to our house plants, too, and remember that even yogurt has feelings. What next?

Shall we communicate by ESP, telepathy, thought wave? By memories of previous incarnations, or via tarot cards and astrology? Let us go anywhere, talk to anything—as long as it is not human. A bodiless mind or a magnetic impulse is easier to communicate with than the spouse, the colleague, the friend, the neighbor next door.

Has anyone calculated the cost of these flights into the empyrean, these conversations with the unearthly? It may seem less expensive than the air fare to a favorite vacation resort, but it is reckoned in a different currency.

Hi-Psi

If there is not yet enough evidence that the national mind is stumbling, if not actually tottering, consider the current enthusiasm for the world of Psi, psychic phenomena.

This is now enjoying a revival surpassing the era of Sir Oliver Lodge in England of the 1880s, when mediums were summoning spirits to tip the tables in the highest intellectual circles, and civil servants in the outposts of the British Empire were sending home other-worldly intelligence reports. They described hair-raising apparitions, telepathic messages, and long-distance murders accomplished by supernaturally gifted aborigines. The editors of the *Journal of Psychical Research* assured their readers that only "dependable" marvels were given the cachet of publication.

So now, a century later, we race around the same course again, with a new set of scientific fripperies in the current mode. We have passed through the brief flurry of Ufology, the study of unidentified flying objects now happily on the wane. Somewhat subdued by the definitive report of the United States Air Force, which dismissed the phenomena as illusory, the followers of UFO or their psychological siblings have found other paranormal pastures to graze in.

Some of them have already staked out their disciplines. Exobiology, metapsychiatry, paraphysics, psychokinesis—note their beautiful names, all derived from Greek in the latest fashion of scientific nomenclature. Note also that none of them has yet found verification in any hard-headed scientific procedure such as controlled or reproducible experiments, for example. But, like the aspirin image makers on TV who wear the white jacket of the man of medicine, they deck themselves in the terminology of science.

Investigations of extrasensory perception have been with us for a long time, and spirit possession, apparitions, hauntings, poltergeists, communication with the dead, and the recapture of memories from previous incarnations go back still further. Now we have people who find time and money to dally in such quaint fields as thoughtography, in which thought processes are said to make pictures on film. We have spirit photography, which claims to capture on the photographic plate the images of those long deceased—and which, by the way, was going on a century ago as well. And we are told of psychic surgery, a procedure in which diseased tissue is excised from the body by mind power alone, without the use of any instruments.

It is all very remarkable, this ground swell of activity in superconscious phenomena. Nearly a hundred colleges and universities are offering their students courses for credit in psychic research. The ESP laboratory of the late Dr. Rhine at Duke University has been polished up and is in full spate. The American Association for the Advancement of Science has admitted to its debates and to its journal professional research workers who are investigating a broad spectrum of paranormal phenomena. While nothing has yet been turned up in this area there is sufficient exuberance to encourage foundations and other grant sources to float such projects.

There are surely deeper reasons than faddism or curiosity for this wave of parascientific excitement. Our security blanket of faith in our social institutions is long since threadbare, and now we are shaken in our trust in the scientists. Far from nurturing our hopes of a healthier, happier world, our men of science have become the new prophets of doom. If they no longer promise us the ultimate nuclear holocaust—to which in a way we have become inured—they now offer us nightmare threats of carcinogenic pollutants in the air we breathe, the water we drink, the plastically packaged foods we buy in our supermarkets.

Recently, they began predicting our destruction by cosmic rays because of the aerosols that they themselves invented and gave us for the innocent uses of perfuming our bodies, deodorizing our dwellings, and spraying away innumerable other nuisances.

What are scientists for, if not to protect us from such disasters? But they do not, apparently cannot, protect us. Instead they haunt our slumber with them. Who needs such scientists, who first create the genies of our destruction and then are helpless to control them? To the devil with them. Let's have no more science, only the illusion of science, which is more fun and less dangerous.

But is it without danger?

Where's the Harm?

For the hyperindividualists, there is a special temptation to roam in this elevated realm of the supermind, this intellectual Hanging Garden of a new Babylon. The hyperindividualists are the characteristic personalities of our waning century, the products of our megalomaniacal technological bureaucracy, and they are most at home in it. They have rejected genuine human involvements, even the deceptive involvements of careless hedonism, and they live in a self-created shell of detachment that to them represents independence and freedom. No matter that they are members of a family, a business community, a neighborhood—they have learned how to live within any group and yet remain isolated and insulated from personal attachments.

Yet one powerful need exists, no matter how they try to suppress it or channel it elsewhere, and that is the need for something more than a merely functional interaction with other human beings. The need to communicate with each other has been built into us since the dawn of mankind. It is no accident that so much of the human brain is devoted to speech, language, reading, and writing, and that another complex system involves the nonverbal brain and indeed the entire body, viscera and all, in the life of the emotions.

Our capacity to communicate, to respond, is part of our original inheritance, our bequest from the first upright humanoid. And although the hyperindividualists cannot acknowledge it, they too are uttering a silent cry in the dark: *Speak to me, listen to me!*

They dare not acknowledge this need, because it undermines the one thing that they have faith in, their independent, self-sufficient selves. And so they look for other times and places, for a new world of people, different and strange, tricked out with superacronyms and superscience.

And ready to oblige them is this fashionable world of the superconscious, with its psychic mysteries, its extrasensory promises, its beckoning to far-out experience, and with the reassuring presence within the movement of a splinter group of scientists, research grants in hand and trailing all the right initials after their names.

For one of these self-sufficient selves, the trip with Supermind came a cropper. She was a young woman, skilled in computer science, trim, attractive, possessed of the ready coin of with-it quips and allusions that keep bubbles of conversation in the air and are guaranteed to forestall any genuine communication. She had a well-paid job as a computer programmer, a pleasant if tiny apartment at a good East Side address, a host of agreeable colleagues and acquaintances. She came to me in a state verging on panic.

She had left home in a West Coast town to go to college and graduate school and had never gone back. One could hardly blame her; it had the sound of a peculiarly sterile, airless environment. Her father was a nonparticipant in family life who spent his leisure hours watching television. Her mother immersed herself in endless charitable projects. Her two sisters, one older and one younger than herself, formed an alliance that excluded her, as sometimes happens to a middle child. She had been a good student, active in high school clubs and games, and had played the flute in high school and college orchestras, but she had never had a really close, special friend. A recruiter for an electronics company had offered her a job during her last year at the university and, armed with her degree and her employment contract, she set out to live her own life in the metropolis.

An invisible part of her baggage was a childhood habit, not surprising in lonely youngsters, of daydreaming. It had never interfered with her studies, and now it did not interfere with her work. Indeed her job, which was largely mechanical, left much of her mind idling and open to fantasizing.

Her colleagues on the job, equally highly trained in

the new technologies, were also equally self-reliant, independent, uninvolved. They talked to their computers and about them as living creatures with thoughts and feelings—this also is not unusual in people working with machines. When they were not talking of computers, their conversation was full of the latest in ESP, thought transference, and the kind of inhabitants that might exist in other galaxies. She sometimes joined some of her colleagues at lectures on psychic phenomena.

In her childhood daydreams she had had imaginary companions, Little People, as many children do at one or another stage of their development. Now in her adult daydreaming they returned, but with a difference. Now they took on some of the quality of her real world of electronics and technology, of space travel and astronomical calculation. From simply imagining someone to talk to, she metamorphosed the playful, childish fantasy into a group of visitors from outer space who became more and more real to her. She had only to stretch out on her bed, in her solitary apartment, and there they were, newly arrived in their space capsule, having come to earth purposely to talk to her, to be the sympathetic friends she did not have in her real life.

She became dependent on her Little People, so wise, so understanding, so safe to confide in. She established a kind of working relationship with them; they could not take her with them to their distant planet, because her earthly body was not strong enough to endure an intergalactic journey, but they would always come back in their spaceship whenever she needed them. There was no problem, of course, in communication. She had only to think of them, and her thought wave would instantly summon them.

Presently, she was summoning them not only in the privacy of her apartment but on the long ride to and from her job in a crowded subway train, and then on the job itself. At first she called them only when she had time to spare between tasks, but soon, and more and more often, they came while she was ostensibly working. She became distracted, began to make mistakes, began to fear for her job. She took increasingly frequent breaks, explaining to her supervisor that she was suffering from dizziness or faintness.

When she came to me, she was ready to acknowledge that matters had gone dangerously out of control. We agreed that the Little People were to remain strictly between us. In subsequent sessions, as she became less frightened and distracted, I encouraged her to return to her music. Gradually she was practicing with better concentration and more regularity on her flute, a most wholesome antidote to daydreaming.

Between her music and her work with me, during which she strove earnestly at disentangling her tangled web of fantasy and reality, she was ultimately able to do without the Little People. Then I did something

I rarely do. Since she was now becoming quite a serious musician, I introduced her to my circle of musical friends. Little by little, meeting new friends and friends of friends, she developed her own small circle of people who were not hyperindividualists and not creatures out of intergalactic space, simply people whom she could communicate with and interest herself in as human beings. She was able to give up not only the Little People but the hyperindividualistic illusion of self-sufficiency, and be herself.

Mystic, Ecstatic

One hesitates to turn a clinical microscope on other people's professed religious experiences. Even William James in his psychological investigations shrank from this field. But the fact is that this era, in which people are literally sickening for something to believe in, is also an era of exotic cults and ecstatic evangelism. There could be a connection.

So I was both impressed and curious when a pastoral psychologist, a professor at the New York Theological Seminary, was courageous enough to make a study of one of the new evangelical manifestations that has swept through the Catholic and the principal Protestant churches, gathering some quarter of a million adherents in the past few years. It is called the "charismatic renewal" or neo-Pentecostal movement, and a significant part of its religious observances is glossolalia, speaking in tongues.

Dr. John Kildahl, an ordained Lutheran clergyman as well as a clinical psychologist, subjected this phenomenon, which the Pentecostal Christians hold to be spiritual and divinely inspired, to investigation under a grant from the National Institute of Health. He concluded that glossolalia was not inspired but learned behavior, and that five conditions were present when people began speaking in tongues for the first time. He listed these conditions as a "magnetic" relationship with a group leader, an intense emotional atmosphere, a supporting group, a prior learning of the religious significance of the experience, and—the one that most interested me—a sense of personal distress.

He described the situations of personal distress as often involving "a fundamental shaking of one's personal and professional identity, with the loss of meaning and purpose for one's existence." Very interesting. And the report went on, "Psychologically, it appears at times that glossolalia serves as the central confirming experience of one's existence."

He noted that most glossolalists seemed to show a greater love for mankind than before their experience. But he also observed some negative consequences, such as a mechanistic dependence on a leader, arrogance, elitism, and "rather histrionic displays of emotion and behavior."

To this an Episcopal rector retorted, "Why is it so strange that if God lives in me He should give me the power to talk in words beyond my understanding?" The conference ended, says *The New York Times*, with a liturgy "marked by speaking and singing in tongues."

Quite so. I still offer no argument with another's religious experience. I simply offer another, and to me antithetical, report. It has nothing to do with glosso-lalia, revival, evangelism, or anything in the preceding account, and it may not even be religious. It is a report of two Jesuit social scientists who sent out a questionnaire to fifteen hundred persons, more or less at random, asking them if they had ever had a mystical experience.

The answer was astonishing. By extrapolation, four out of ten Americans experience one or more mystical episodes in their lives. The description of a mystical experience is difficult to come by, since in its very essence it is nonverbal and does not lend itself to description in words. Those who were believers described it in their answers to the questionnaire as a sense of the presence of God. Others spoke of being lifted out of themselves, of becoming part of something greater. But for all, or almost all, the experience was bright and beneficent, a confirmation of the goodness of life.

Now we come to what was, for me, the most interesting part of the report. The people who answered yes, that they had had such an experience or more than one, were comfortable members of society. Many were churchgoers but not especially religious. None had expected or sought the experience, nor was it drug- or otherwise induced. And none—or so I deduced from the report—was "in distress."

And there I rest my case, if there is a case, that the pure mystical experience, whether or not it is divinely inspired, does not need to be sought. The capability for it seems to be present in that largely unexplored continent, the human psyche. Primitive man made this discovery in himself. And my further point is that it is indeed a pure experience, not related to either psychological or existential distress.

But, once having discovered that such an experience is possible, human beings have not been content to let it happen. They have been seeking it for centuries, for millennia.

They are seeking it again today, and somewhat frantically. Hundreds of thousands of Americans are experimenting with induced mystical experience, not for the experience itself, but in the mistaken belief that it will resolve their existential dilemmas or deliver them from their profound personal malaise.

This therapeutic notion probably all began with psychedelic drug research and around a great man of letters, Aldous Huxley. Consciousness-expanding became the game that began with chemicals, then shifted to the control of body states by mind manipulation.

Recently, it has surfaced again with much the same passionate faddism, with a décor sometimes ritualistic, sometimes scientific.

A school of psychology explains these experiences as arising in the right hemisphere of the brain—or, for the left-handed, the left hemisphere—which has participated little if at all in the hard-driving rationalism of the Western world. The theory is provocative, but it does not easily lend itself to experimental proof and so, like it or not, it remains largely speculative, neither proved nor disproved.

The forms it takes in its present popular resurgence are mostly derived from Eastern religions since we in the West have ignored and denigrated this part of the mind for centuries. The most widely advertised form is meditation.

From TV to TM

Probably an improvement over the six hours a day, or whatever the average is, that Americans supposedly spend before their television sets, is the new mode of escape by way of transcendental meditation, or TM, as it is cosily known to its practitioners, who now number some four hundred thousand in this country. I read that this is a worldwide movement but that it is especially strong in the United States, that its devotees embrace all ages and vocations, and that 350 centers across the country teach the practice to ten thousand novices a month.

Meditation was known in ancient Egypt and is practiced by contemporary Eskimos. Over the centuries it has been cultivated by Hindus, Buddhists, and the Japanese masters of Zen, by the Sufis of Islam and the early Christians, by the Talmudic sages in Jerusalem and Babylon, and by the cabalists and alchemists of medieval Europe.

I do not argue, as some do, that because it comes to us from exotic sources it has no place in the psyche of Western man. We can learn from the ancients and the East, and it would be sheer hubris to claim that our vast technology is a substitute for the fruits of contemplation harvested through the millennia by holy or dedicated men.

But consider the nature of our existence in the world of today. Each of us is the product of our culture, our nurture, and—give or take a few—our genes. For most of us mere survival is not enough, although for a large number necessity still places inexorable limits on experience. Each of us is engaged on a pilgrimage through life, and as to its goals, doubts may arise that are grave enough to fell a man or woman in the prime of life. Many of us in our middle years are confronted with the terrible fear that we have wandered off course and our fretful journey has been for naught.

People who come to such a crossroads surely need

signposts to turn them from the dead-end byways down which they have been led by their culture or their nurture, and guide them instead toward a rational way of dealing with the uncertainties and inequities of their real world. For such a course, no "new consciousness" is required, only the full use of the consciousness they have, the reasoning, understanding, value-weighing mind. To unravel the self from fantasy and illusion, to see it naked and not through the prisms of conformity and pretense—that can hardly be achieved in a state of chemically or metabolically produced "nothingness."

But that is precisely what some of the devotees of transcendental meditation claim for it, that learning to empty the mind to the point of mental void, of no mind at all, will cure their psychic pains and send them through life healed and liberated. If only they did not claim so much!

For there is no question that meditation has its uses. Its technique lies in the cultivation of another mode of operation of the nervous system than the one by which we ordinarily operate. The Eastern cults achieve their control of this in various ways. Some concentrate on gazing steadily at a religious diagram, a mandala, said to be charged with psychic energy, and some settle for fixing the gaze on any secular object, a vase, a candle, a piece of fruit. Some repetitiously chant a prayer or a simple sound. The transcendental meditation teachers supply—for a fee—a mantra, a sound of one or two syllables, said to be especially designed for the individual and which is to be disclosed to no one. Repetition of this sound, either voiced or silent, leads to the objective, which is the same in all techniques, the exclusion of thought.

Or, as one guru told a pupil who traveled six thousand miles to learn his secret, "Sit facing the wall and count your breaths. That is all." That was the sum total of his instruction.

Zen teachers offer a paradox or riddle, a koan, on which the pupil is to meditate. Current gurus have creatively packaged new koans for modern Americans, such as, "What is the size of the real you?" and "How can I attain enlightenment by driving on the freeway?" This last seems to me a highly hazardous exercise if practiced *in situ*—that is, on the freeway.

There is a classic koan, introduced decades ago by the Zen sage of Columbia University, the late Dr. Suzuki, and by Erich Fromm, "What is the sound of one hand clapping?" This is so popular in meditation circles that it has become a one-liner on television comedy shows, and we may expect soon to see it on the movie screen, with a comedian in the role of the other hand.

Since riddles are now a part of the Consciousness Revolution, I also have a riddle to suggest, hand-lettered by one of my patients and presented to me. It says:

"I know that you believe you understand what you

think I said, but I am not sure you realize that what you heard is not what I meant."

That is an existential riddle, and also worth meditating on.

Be Kind to Your SNS

There can be little question that certain sonorities, plucked out of the cacophony of our times, can enlarge our sense of ourselves and generate refreshing energy. After a day of fruitless wrangling in courtrooms or conference rooms, listening to a little Mozart can quiet quivering nerves. An aching day of teaching obstreperous adolescents can be soothed by a sauna and a cold plunge. After a traffic-clogged, gas-polluted drive, a solitary walk can thaw congealed senses.

To each his own relief from stress, his own path to calm and perhaps to ecstasy. They are short-term measures we learn to take against situational pressures, modes of recovery from psychophysical imbalance. They do not solve a single one of the continuing problems of our existence in the real world. They are antidotes, not panaceas.

Who says that altering the operation of our nervous system or the physiology of our breathing will release us from the grip of our unproductive fantasies and confusions? Who says that gazing at a vase or an apple, or repeating "om," or thinking of nothing, for forty minutes every day can liberate us from hating our work, detesting our spouse, being compulsively attracted to noise, alcohol, or sex, or lapsing into enervating dependency needs?

Can the Superconscious really raise the level of life? Do the spirits of an Indian guru or Carlos Castaneda's Don Juan have telephone numbers? Would they answer a call for help from one whose hopes are so low that suicide beckons, whose frustrations have the taste of gall?

In our world, meditation may have a direct physiological usefulness in its effect on the sympathetic nervous system, the SNS. This is differentiated from the CNS, the central nervous system, which brings us information through our senses and operates our muscles. The SNS operates the heart, viscera, glands. It is what goes haywire under certain kinds of stress and gives us stomach ulcers, asthma, and a number of other unpleasant ills. It functions automatically to raise and lower blood pressure and heart rate.

At a threat of physical or psychic harm, the SNS sets in motion the fight-or-flight reaction. It pours adrenalin into the blood, accelerates breathing and pulse, alerts the muscles. It dilates the pupils of our eyes—so we can better see the enemy, or the escape route—and it sets everything, including our teeth, on edge if in fact we can neither fight nor run away in, for example, a confrontation with the boss, the spouse, the landlord, or whomever. The fight-or-flight reaction, a lifesaving mechanism in the jungle, was considered by Dr. Franz Alexander one of the prime causes of cardiovascular and —yes—arthritic ailments because it is chronically stimulated and at the same time frustrated in our Western civilization.

So what we find, in carefully monitored laboratory studies of meditation, is that this technique is in demonstrable ways an antidote to the fight-or-flight response. Using the full scientific array, research physiologists have found that oxygen intake, blood pressure, and heart action subside, skin resistance rises (it is low under stress), and certain stress-related chemicals in the blood decline, all at rates significantly higher even than in ordinary sleep.

By the phenomenon that today we call biofeedback, some subjects skilled in these exercises seem consciously able to reduce the rate of all these sympathetic nervous system responses. Serious physiologists have begun paying heed to this phenomenon, the same that enables yoga masters to walk barefoot on burning coals or to bury themselves in boxes or sandpits.

But up to now, biofeedback as a way of curing high blood pressure or cardiac problems is not even a dream. No sufferer from these ailments can safely substitute meditation for medication. The biofeedback exercises are so far little more than interesting parlor games.

By the same token, meditation, whether transcendental or any other brand, is no substitute for the reality testing of responsible therapy. But it may provide, for those who like to try it, a short-term antidote for the tensions and anxieties of the ordinary daily round, a kind of psychophysiological respite.

A reporter who dutifully paid her $125 for instruction and a personal and private mantra found that by resolutely setting aside twenty minutes twice each day she did achieve relaxation of her muscular tensions and a degree of inner calm. Her husband, who got his method for free from a physiologist's laboratory experiment (his device was to intone the word "one" on each exhaled breath) enjoyed similar agreeable comforts.

Another TM practitioner was relieved (she said "cured") of her lower back pain, and then discovered that by simply moving from New York City to a quieter town she no longer felt the need to meditate. Another meditator said he definitely felt less anxious. Still another, a woman engaged in a high-pressure business in a high-pressure metropolis, said that she was careful not to exceed the prescribed forty minutes daily because if she meditated longer she began to experience hallucinations. The hallucinations were not in themselves frightening—she saw birds, flowers, fountains—but she did not like being in a hallucinatory state.

As to that, the wise men of the East have already warned us. During the first and second centuries the rabbis of Jerusalem, writing the Talmud and its companion volume of wisdom, the Mishnah, told the story of four sages who, while meditating on the throne of

God, found themselves transported to paradise. At the sight of the heavenly glories, the first of the four was struck dead, the second went mad, the third became a heretic. Only the fourth, the great scholar Rabbi Akiba, "ascended in peace and descended in peace."

To those who expect to meditate their way to a paradise free from earthly cares, I offer this cautionary tale together with its historical epilogue. Rabbi Akiba, who alone returned safely from his blissful heavenly journey, went on to become one of Judaism's sainted martyrs, tortured to death by the Romans for his part in the Bar Kokba rebellion.

Even a sage could not—or perhaps would not—escape from the existential realities of his time.

Nor would he abandon, even to save his life, the other human beings with whom he had lived it. He was like the intellectuals of occupied France two millennia later who joined the Resistance against the Nazis; he was *l'homme engagé*, a man engaged in living with his kind.

Fortunately for the rest of us, we are not ordinarily called upon to be heroes or martyrs. But we may remember with Rabbi Akiba that although we may glimpse paradise, we live our lives on earth as human beings among other human beings, and we realize our humanity fully only as we link our lives with others.

- *In a crazy world, it is plausible to expect many crazy therapies.*

- *We cut ourselves off from real people—and then invent unreal ones to take their place.*

- *A flight into fantasy had better have a rational navigator along for the return trip.*

- *Oriental disciplines may expand the mind, but don't count on them for an Occidental life-support system.*

- *We can learn from the sages. They dreamed dreams and saw visions, but they lived in the real world among real people.*

The Rose-Garden Children

6

Some people say they are emotionally infantile, some say they have a chronic case of the gimmes, and some say they are just plain spoiled rotten and a social nuisance.

I call them the rose-garden children, because they are still looking for a world their childhood taught them to expect, a world full of loving people who will cater to their needs, shelter them from grief and pain, and while strewing rose petals in their path, will fulfill their every wish.

They are now men and women in their thirties or nearing forty. Some have children, and many of them have been in and out of several marriages. Whatever they may say or believe about themselves, they are not doing well. To put it bluntly, they are a pain in the neck to everyone around them, and sometimes even to themselves.

Invariably, as if it were the same recorded message, they tell me tales of blighted hopes and expectations, of disappointments in people they trusted, of failed relationships. Some express feelings of near desperation. Whether they are married or living with a partner in quasi-marriage, or surrounded with friends and family, the one feeling all of them express is that of being deeply, painfully lonely.

And I am obliged to tell them, at some proper time, that there is no comfort for their loneliness, because what they are seeking—in love, marriage, friendship, or any relationship at all—is something that does not exist, that their child's world with all its wishes and whims fulfilled can never be recaptured.

The rose-garden children are also among the "new people," but they are not to be confused with those cool hyperindividualists who reject all human relationships except functional ones, and rely only on themselves. The so-called spoiled rotten children are also egocentric, but their egocentricity, unlike that of children, has no charm for us. We become impatient, annoyed, angry, or simply bored. For, when they try to please, their efforts are shallow and transparent; they are only playing for the reward, the lollipop or ice cream cone for a good child. But their demands are not the small wants of children. Theirs are adult demands, exorbitant and tyrannical. And if they are refused, their hurt and indignation may be monumental.

They are not aware of any of this. They do not know that they are attempting blackmail. They feel that they are loving and ask only to be loved in return. They are deaf to the sounds of others' needs and wishes, cannot hear them for the clamor of their own. And—as is obvious to people who deal with children—the greater a child's hunger for love, the less lovable the child. With forty-year-old children, their lovability is in the same inverse ratio.

Scars of the Child-Centered Family

Yet, their suffering is real, and it can be understood and explained. They are the grown-up children of the child-centered family of a generation ago, and they bear the scars of that extraordinary and peculiar aberration of child-rearing philosophy.

It was a transient period, from about the middle 1930s through the 1950s, during which parents saw themselves as having been put on earth for only one purpose—to make their children happy. Mothers went about with Dr. Spock's book in one hand and books of child psychology and parent education in the other. Fathers impoverished themselves to give their children the finest education, from nursery school through university. Parents spent tortured hours in profound psychological analyses of every act of childish waywardness.

They reasoned with their children as did Plato with his students in the groves of Academe. They seized upon every childish interest, nurtured every random whim of childhood as if they had struck gold. They cheerfully gave up their own vacation trips to send their children to riding camps, sailing camps, music camps, and expensive artsy-craftsy retreats for gifted children.

All this was in reaction against a long history of calculated—or sometimes unavoidable—neglect of children by parents or society. In Victorian times a good child was seen and not heard, and not even seen too often. It was a world in which parents served their own interests first and last. They traveled abroad with numerous pieces of luggage, leaving the children like another batch of luggage to the care of others. If the children received the Tom Brown treatment while the parents were off on the grand tour—well, that was good for the children's souls and bodies. The purgatory of an English public school is something that even a prince of Wales is expected to endure. In this country, there were times when a male child who did not work for his pocket money was considered a ne'er-do-well who would come to no good end.

How Sharper Than a Serpent's Tooth . . .

No doubt the child-centered generation created beautiful Peter Pan lives for the offspring who, now grown, are so desperately trying to retrieve that childhood paradise. A more subtle consequence is that those parents, by their sacrificial exertions, laid on their children an intolerable burden. Spoken or unspoken, conscious or unconscious, the expectation was that the child would make a return to the parent by becoming a superachiever—a brilliant diplomat, a merchant prince, a Nobel scientist, or perhaps a psychoanalyst—and thus live out the parent's hopes, dreams, and aspirations for him.

No wonder the children of the middle sixties rebelled. No wonder so many of them fled geographically and ideologically as far as they could from their parents. No wonder they dropped out, traveled in packs to Europe, to India, to Tibet, and sat down to await the arrival of American Express money orders from parents quivering with anxiety.

Of course, there were other causes for the children's rebellion. The sequence of wars, assassinations, and breakdowns of the institutions of civilization contributed to their rejection of the entire adult world, including their parents.

But I find that the rose-garden children who today are

struggling through the crucial years of their own adulthood are not complaining about world disasters. They are wrestling with elusive ghosts of a remembered paradise, fighting shadows in the dark of their own blindness. And, for their struggles, they receive nothing but wounding blows from the people around them, who perceive them as wrinkled children incapable of coping very well.

Many rose-garden children are not even veterans of the great rebellion. A mother told me of an exchange between her husband and her son in his late twenties. This son had stayed on course, had sat out the rebellion right through college and graduate school, and his father, not a rich man, was offering him a trip to Europe. The young man, usually gentle and soft-spoken, exploded in wild rage. "I don't want a trip to Europe! I don't want your damn money! I'll go to Europe when I damn well want to go, and I'll pay for it myself!" he shouted.

The mother, telling me this, expressed shock. "Shouldn't he have thanked his father, at least, for the generous offer?" And she added, with the characteristic guilt of the child-centered parent, "What did we do wrong, that he should burst out in such a rage?"

What she failed to grasp was that the young man did not feel thankful, that he was resentful, rather, over the long history of being protected and sustained and guided, long after he should have felt free to go his own way. He was fighting against being smothered by their excessive generosity, and fighting, too, against his own fear of being seduced again, back into the soft world of childhood. He was clinging with all his might to his barely won adulthood and he had no time, standing shakily on the brink, to be civil to his father.

I remember another story, this time told me by a daughter. She had accepted travel to Europe, study in foreign universities, and finally a graduate course in an American university that would equip her for a teaching career. Midway in her studies, she abandoned her courses in pedagogy and switched to studio courses in pottery making. This time it was the father who was angry.

"What are you doing out there in that expensive graduate school, piddling around with clay?" he demanded. "You're supposed to be working for a teaching certificate so you can earn a living!"

She said to me with some indignation, "What do you think of that? He was paying for graduate school—but with strings attached!"

Never mind that the attached string was intended to give her economic independence. That part of the bargain she did not acknowledge, had not even heard when the bargain was first made. Economic independence, or any kind of independence, was what she precisely did not want, what in fact she was terrified of. Her father was the angel with the flaming sword, driving her from the Garden of Eden. And, indeed, she and her father could never have understood each other, because they were speaking different languages. He spoke with the voice of existential reality—from which, to be sure, he had shielded her all those years—but the only voices she could hear were those of her fantasy world.

So much for the deserved rewards of parental sacrifice, the protective love that lays larvae to be hatched later in open hostility. But that was ten and fifteen years ago. What is hurting these grown-up refugees from the child-centered world today?

The Unisex Lovers

The young woman sat in my office. Besides a pert, pretty face and a charming figure, she had a freshly scrubbed look of health and vitality that no cosmetics or beauty treatments can duplicate. She was a delight to the eyes and an irresistible invitation to any normally sexed young man.

And then, still composed, still smiling, she dropped a grenade. She told me that she had been married to a husband she loved for three and a half years, and they had never had sex together.

Why? Was he not well? Did he not love her? She shook her head at both questions. He was young, strong, athletic, as she was. He loved her as she loved him. They were always together. They swam, skated, skied, danced, played tennis, always together. They enjoyed the same plays, movies, concerts, books. They were perfect companions. "He's everything I could dream of in a husband," she said.

Except for sex. They kissed affectionately, held hands, went to sleep in each other's arms. But when it came to sex, he was simply not interested. He felt no sexual urgency at all. He was happy with things as they were, and could not see any reason to change.

She, too, had been content—until recently. Recently she had become restless, had found herself looking speculatively at other men, having sexual fantasies about other men. This troubled her. She did not approve of infidelity, did not want to hurt her husband. What should she do?

What she should do was not the first question that needed answering. How did such a situation come about?

I met her husband, and he was everything she had said he was, a perfect match for her in looks and a charming, witty fellow besides. In fact they looked surprisingly like each other, and when I mentioned this, she laughed and told me that until recently people could hardly tell them apart. They had worn identical jeans and sweaters, had their hair cut the same way, had looked like a pair of girlish boys or boyish girls. "You know, the unisex thing," she explained. And what had happened recently? She shrugged. "Well, I changed my style. I began to wear skirts."

I further learned that they had been living all this time in his mother's apartment. Oh, not with his mother!

When they married, that considerate mother, who happened to be widowed, had simply moved out into a smaller place and had given them her cooperative apartment, fully furnished.

This little bride was cooking in her mother-in-law's kitchen with her mother-in-law's pots and pans, serving dinner to her husband in her mother-in-law's dishes, and if she broke one—"Oh, you've broken one of mother's good dinner plates!" She could not change the color of the draperies, the upholstery—"Mother has such perfect taste." She slept with her husband in his mother's bed, between his mother's sheets, and it would have been surprising if they could make love, not that they couldn't.

There was no friction. This admirable mother-in-law never interfered, was always considerate and charming. She treated them both as her children. In giving them her apartment, she had thought only of their comfort. They both had jobs, but on what they earned they could never have afforded a sumptuous establishment on New York's East Side.

This mother's only fault was that she was too thoughtful of her son's comfort. She was still mothering him, still shielding him from the harsh winds of reality in her luxurious downy nest.

We have seen many examples of parents pampering their children to death. I know a man who gave his only child, his daughter, as a wedding present a mansion that her husband could not possibly maintain, and then gave her an allowance to maintain it, until the husband rebelled and the marriage broke up in bitterness. The daughter never recovered from the failure of her marriage, and has lived a joyless life of amorous adventures ever since.

In the case of our unisex couple, the mothering has gone to an extreme that would be comic if it were not sad. The young man is obviously sexually retarded—in clinical terms, pre-Oedipal—and it is a question whether his bride, who was rather a slow developer herself, can restrain her newly discovered womanhood long enough for him to catch up, provided he wants to catch up.

It is hard to see why he should want to. He lives in a child's paradise, with a mother to see to his comfort, a delightful girl playmate. As he himself said, what reason would he have to change? Unless, of course, he wants to keep his girl playmate, who—unfortunately for him—is outgrowing his Peter Pan world and becoming a woman. What will be their future? I can guess, but I am a physician, not a fortuneteller.

The Slave-Wife

And here is another marriage of two rose-garden children. The husband, a research physicist, never knew his father. His parents were divorced when he was a baby, and his mother devoted herself to his care. The wife was also a child of over-solicitous parents, and despite a fine education and considerable ability, during the years after college she never sought a professional career, never even applied for a job that was up to her capacity. She had been looking for a husband since she was eighteen. When they met, he courted her assiduously, acceded to all her wishes—"Whatever you want to do . . . Anything you say . . ." It was like her parents all over again, and she was ecstatically happy.

As soon as they married, the climate changed. She had grown up with Beethoven and Bach, but he loved rock and country music, so their house was loud with rock and country music. She loved good plays and movies, but he liked to drink beer and talk shop with his colleagues, so she spent her evenings serving beer and listening to technical discussions of which she understood not one word in three. If she uttered a mild protest, he would look hurt and say, "If you loved me, you would like doing what I like to do."

And, as sometimes happens, she who had always been indulged became the indulgent one. In her fantasy she had changed places with her parents, and was dutifully giving what she longed in her heart to receive. The core of her self became flabby, then weightless, as she accommodated in every aspect of their life—in choice of food, of furniture, of recreation, of sexual practices—so that soon she was sucked into the vortex of her spouse's egocentricity. She became a slave-wife, smiling with clenched teeth while she secretly yearned for the rose garden of her childhood.

Then her body spoke up and began to make the protest she could not yet bring herself to make, in the form of a series of classic gastric upsets. To her husband her illnesses were a deliberate personal affront, and she did her best to get better. But instead she got steadily worse, and finally—to his outraged astonishment—she left him.

Since their divorce he has not changed. He still expects every woman he lives with to conform to his style and his preferences, unable to make allowances for any preferences of hers, and so they leave him, one after the other. His manipulative approach to other human beings disqualifies him for any lasting relationship.

Rose-garden children never find what they are seeking, because they are still looking, not for a partner in life, but for an embodiment of their fantasy, an imaginary father or mother that never really existed. Each is trying to recapture a lost childhood in which every wish was granted—or so, in glowing memory, it appears to them. The only thing to do with such a fantasy is to eschew all relationship with reality, lock oneself into a cork-lined room, and convert it into a literary masterpiece, like Marcel Proust. Or, of course, give up the fantasy for the real world.

The Crying Girl

This rose-garden child was thirty-one, tall, slender, and as the French put it *jolie-laide*, "beautiful-ugly." She could look so striking when she wished that she had no trouble attracting men and even women friends. She had a father, mother, sister, brother, a young child, and even her husband whom she had divorced was still friendly to her. She had her master's degree and was working as a schoolteacher.

But on her visits to my office she sat crumpled in a chair like a child, wearing an old sweater and jeans, no make-up, her hair an unbrushed tangle, and she cried from beginning to end of the session. "I'm so lonely, so terribly lonely!" was her theme.

Here was the loneliness of the grown-up rose-garden child in an extreme form—as doctors often say to each other with apparent heartlessness, a beautiful case. What they mean, of course, is that it is a beautiful example, a textbook case.

She said, "My father is forever giving me money—money, money, money, all the time." She said this with a curious gesture of her two hands, making circles like a mill grinding out money.

I said, "Yes, I suppose he gives you money because he hates you."

At that she slumped still further down into her chair. "Of course, I'm a shit, I'm nothing but a piece of shit."

In the next breath she was a princess. She said of her fellow schoolteachers, "They're dull, dreary, stupid people. I can run rings around them. . . ." So she was both a shit and a princess among the peasants, alternately wallowing in self-disgust and swaggering with the confidence that she was a superior species of human being. This is, of course, no contradiction, merely opposite sides of the same coin.

What was wrong with this grown-up child was her expectation. The circular gesture she had made with her hands was symbolic of more than money. The people around her—family, husband, friends, colleagues —circled around her but could not break through the barrier of her childish fantasy. She herself was circling around and around in her unreal world, unaware even of people's willingness to give her the kindness and affection she craved. In her own eyes she was either too far above them, or too far below. She was either repulsively unworthy of love, or worthy of something far better than any of them could give her.

Let us first of all understand that her loneliness, while extreme, was not neurotic. It was existential loneliness, the loneliness that is intrinsic to the human condition. Every one of us is alone in his own skin, and the ultimate loneliness, the one we all live with, is our mortality. It is an existential fact that we each live and die alone.

Most of us are not walled in with this fact of our humanity. We form connections with each other. We give and receive affection, reassurance, love. But the rose-garden children are so encapsulated in their childhood fantasy of love that they cannot recognize adult human love when it is offered them. What they are looking for is love with no strings attached, love that makes no judgments and demands nothing in return.

But there is no love without strings attached. Even divine love is not absolute. Even God's love has strings attached. If it is the Jehovah of the Old Testament, we must have no other gods and obey the Ten Commandments to win His love. If it is Jesus, we must love our neighbor, turn the other cheek, and believe in Him. A father or mother must set standards for a child's behavior, in order for the child to live as a member of the family and the society. A husband or wife must make demands, because he and she are also human beings and they have human failings and human needs.

There is a description of absolute love. It is in Paul's first Epistle to the Corinthians, Chapter 13, and we are all familiar with it—"Though I speak with the tongues of men and of angels, and have not love, I am become as sounding brass." And it goes on, "Love is kind and patient, Love bears all things, believes all things, forgives all things, endures all things."

That is the kind of love that as children we all crave, and as adults we all know is an ideal, but not a reality that we can expect in life. What the rose-garden children have failed to learn, what they must eventually learn, is that love is indeed an exchange, something that is given as well as received. Friendship and love can begin small, with no more than a recognition of the other's existence, a willingness to be interested in the other as a fellow human being. The rose-garden children have not yet learned to be interested in anyone but themselves.

As adults we also know that the love we give and receive is imperfect, as we are imperfect. And to know that is a relief—which of us feels capable of giving, perfect, absolute love? Or even of receiving it? The very thought of the obligation it would lay on us is intolerable.

But the love that we can give and receive is real, however flawed. And it can warm us, body and spirit, as no fantasied love can ever do.

And the rose-garden children? Their search for a lost paradise is fruitless, because if it ever existed outside of their fantasy it is gone with childhood and can never be regained. If they want surcease from their loneliness, they will find it where the rest of us find it—in the shared world of mutually equal relationships with others.

- *Who ever said parents were put on earth to make children happy?*

- *The erotic life of grown-up rose-garden children tends to have more thorns than roses.*

- *Some adults are merely wrinkled children.*

- *The lost paradise of childhood existed only in fantasy and can only be regained in the same place.*

- *Just as a slight change in attitude can prevent a space capsule from flying off course, so can a minuscule change of attitude keep the psyche from flying into uncharted space.*

- *The danger of trying to recapture a lost childhood is that you may succeed.*

- *Some people take a lifetime to get over once having been children.*

- *Best be prepared to pay for what you get—even God's love is not without a price.*

The Existential Road

In Defense of Uniqueness

7

Every day in my consulting room I hear the same theme, sometimes articulated, sometimes only implied. The man who says, "Dammit, am I some kind of money-making machine to gratify all of my wife's expensive tastes?" The woman who says, "I'm no sexual service station for my husband, nor am I a wailing wall where he can come and cry about all the rotten luck he has. . . ." The grown children who say, "I'm not my parents' little kid any more, to be told how to run my

121

life. . . ." The parents who ask, "Do I have to drop everything and come running, every time they send out a call for help?"

What they are all saying is, "I'm not a function serving some other person's wish or need, not a tool to be used, to be manipulated. I'm me, myself! Why can't they see me as I am, a person separate from themselves, an individual, not like anybody else, only like myself?"

It is both the triumph and the sickness of our Western world, this defense of our individuality, our uniqueness. And, of course, each of us is indeed unique. We all share the same body structure, the same body functions, but each one of us is full of individual anomalies. Each of us has bones and joints that are put together a little differently, blood chemistry that is a little different.

You could search the whole world and not find one human being who is your exact physical counterpart, unless you are an identical twin, and even twins may have their slight disparities although they came from the same egg. Who knows whether the egg divided precisely in half, or if one twin got a little more, the other a little less, of the original supply? And then there were possible environmental differences, even in the womb, in which the growing space and the life-giving blood supply may not have been identically shared. Nature sets down her laws for a viable organism, but with plenty of leeway for the random difference so long as it does not stray too far from the norm. One twin is almost always a little bigger, stronger, quicker, than the other. No two children in the same family grow up in exactly the same environment.

And, if we do not even have the same blood and bones, what shall we say of our intellect, our emotions, our capabilities, the unfathomed mysteries of the psyche? Certainly it is true that each one of us is individual, is unique. The question is, How far do we want to push this uniqueness? How individual does each of us want, or need, to be?

Individualism is supposed to have been born with the Renaissance. I date it much further back, from a man with a long sad face, narrow shoulders, and a pot belly, who according to our modern medical criteria was probably suffering from a hormonal deficiency. This unprepossessing man happened to be the ruler of one of the great nations of his time, and he happened also to have as a wife one of the most beautiful women of all time. He was Ikhnaton, who became pharaoh of Egypt 3,375 years ago.

He has come down to us in history, not because he was the husband of the incomparable Nefertiti, but because he was the first man in history to proclaim that there was only one god. Not for him the ram-headed Amen or any of the ibis-headed, jackal-headed, hawk-headed gods of Egypt. His god stood alone, beyond earth and its creatures—the beneficent, life-giving sun.

The First Individualist

The priests of Amen made short work of this new religion after Ikhnaton's death, which indeed they may have hastened. They destroyed his city and his temples, defaced his monuments, and tried to erase him from history. But they could not destroy all the papyri in the tombs, which have given us some of the most beautiful hymns to the one god. Nor could they destroy all the art that he inspired in his brief seventeen-year reign, the first humanistic paintings and sculptures in the world. In them we see not the conventionalized identical figures and faces of three thousands years of Egyptian art, but uniquely individual human beings. We see Nefertiti with her swanlike throat and exquisite features, and the drooping, intellectual Ikhnaton himself.

Moses, who led the Israelites out of Egypt some fifty years—give or take a few decades—after Ikhnaton's death, made the one God even more remote than the sun. Indeed he moved God right out of the universe, an invisible deity of whom no likeness could be made. Whatever the Yahweh of Abraham may have been—a tribal god, or, as some scholars believe, a mountain deity borrowed from some neighboring people—the one God of Moses was ineffable. When Genesis came to be written down perhaps two thousand years later, this vision of the remote deity was fixed as the Creator who could be known only through His creation, and the lord of that creation was man, made in God's image.

With such a deity, ordinary human beings could have no intimacy. But, if they were created in his image, instead of intimacy each man had in himself something of the divine being. Each man had in himself a personal, individual share of divinity.

For about the first fifteen hundred years of the Christian Era in Europe, no one had much time to be concerned about his individuality. To the Church the fragment of the divine in each man was his immortal soul, and men worried mainly about the fate of their souls in the eternity after death. A few highly individualistic characters are known to us—the ragged, rascally, divinely ironic poet François Villon, the regal Eleanor of Aquitaine who bequeathed to us the fiction of courtly or romantic love from which we are not yet entirely liberated, and the remarkable Frederick II, called the Wonder of the World, whose court in Sicily brought the scholars, scientists, and mathematicians, mostly Arabic and Jewish, to leaven the thought of medieval Europe.

There were also a few philosophers like Saint Augustine and Moses Maimonides, a few poets like Dante and Chaucer. But most of the individualists of the Middle Ages were artists and artisans who could not even write their names, but were content to contribute their unique visions and the unique skills of their hands to the glory of God in the churches and cathedrals, without individual billing in the historical record.

The Renaissance changed all that. Artists, writers, explorers, scientists, inventors all learned to sign their names to their work. Each man felt possessed not only of his own divine spark but also of the power to assert it. And ever since, in our Western world, each one of us has been promised the opportunity—or burdened with the responsibility, if you prefer—to sign our names somewhere, somehow, as proof of our individual existence.

In America the drive for individual existence became a drive for individual achievement—"rugged individualism," as it came to be called. Linked to economic achievement, it gradually lost its humane character. The spark of God in each man spurred him to take for himself as much as he could grasp of wealth and glory. In the rush for power, farmers and artisans, the once proud individualists, faded into the faceless population of factory hands. Art was ground into the commercial assembly line. Advertising dictated uniform tastes and appetites. Big business, big government, big education and their faithful tools, the bureaucracies, diminished the individual to the vanishing point. Then came the computer to reduce him to punch cards and digits.

And so we have the reaction, a reassertion of human individuality, of divine uniqueness. And this is where the existential road begins, which I call the road to freedom.

How Much Uniqueness?

The reaction against achievement and in favor of uniqueness began several decades ago. Carl Gustav Jung first made it the center of his therapy, calling it "individuation." Carl Rogers and Abraham Maslow independently took the same direction with "self-actualization." And the thousands who attend encounter groups are each presumably in search of his own and her own unique identity, unique individuality.

Meanwhile, the power structures of our time grow ever more voracious in their need for people as computer numbers rather than as individuals, our urban and suburban communities become ever more regimented and identical, and even our escapes from all this take on an anti-individual pattern. The young people in the counterculture of the 1960s sought their individual identity, ironically, in identical clothes, hair styles, pop songs, cults, and drug abuse. The liberated women moved out of the sex-symbol uniform into the uniform of uncoiffed hair, face bare of make-up, and the identical ideology and jargon of the movement. Uniqueness, it appears, is harder to win and easier to lose than the Christian's state of grace or the politician's state of democracy.

So we must ask ourselves, Is there such a quality as uniqueness? Who is unique? And even more troubling are such questions as, Do we want to be unique? How much of an individual, how different from our fellows, does any of us really want to be?

Perhaps our individuality is just another fantasy of the Western world, like Eleanor of Aquitaine's romantic love. Perhaps it is not realizable even in the smallest degree. Norbert Wiener pointed out that, like nature, human society also tends to follow the second law of thermodynamics and reduce us all to an undifferentiated equilibrium. Certainly the forces, both external and internal, seem to press in that direction. It is so much more comfortable just to go along with the stream.

The majority of people are content to do just that, and always have been. Most people have accepted their place in life and gone quietly about their business of being serf or lordling, peasant or craftsman, parish priest or merchant. Today they are the blue-collar and white-collar workers, the unemployed or unemployable on welfare, the sales people and service people and middle- and top-management people. More and more the doctors, lawyers, architects, and even psychiatrists follow identical patterns as members of the service class.

Yet, even among the most numerous and least identifiable people we see the thrust of a need to be identified. We see it in the grafitti—someone out there wants to sign his name. We read it in the newspaper accounts of violence—someone out there found a way to sign his name in blood.

In our modern Western world we also have the illusion and sometimes the reality of upward mobility. The medieval peasant and his feudal lord had no such illusion. They knew they would live out their lives in the status to which they were born. But we in our society are encouraged to think we can improve our status, or at least change it.

And so we struggle, with education, with cunning, with the aspirations and aid of our parents, to do so. What we mainly accomplish is to exchange one pattern of life for another. We exchange the label we were born to for the label of the man or woman on the next socioeconomic level—from garage mechanic to auto salesman to head of the agency, from a smaller to a bigger and bigger house in a more expensive suburb, from a smaller to a bigger car or two or three.

The man who has made it to wealth and status may feel himself unique. He has signed his name. From the hustler in pursuit of "contacts" he has become the "contact" the hustlers pursue. What has he gained? And what has it cost him?

A Look at the Price Tag

A man who had "made it" by the age of forty came to see me. He had been the head of his own advertising agency, earning his $150,000 to $200,00 a year. He had signed his name, all right—his agency bore it, unmistakable witness to his uniqueness.

He worked days, nights, and weekends to stay there, when one night, closing his attaché case at midnight and going up to bed, he went past the bedroom shared by his two older sons and heard someone crying. He stopped to listen. The youngest of the three, the ten-year-old, was in the room with his two brothers and it was the youngest one's voice he heard.

"If at least we were orphans!" the child was saying between sobs. "Then we'd know, okay, we haven't got a father. But we've got a father, and we haven't got one!"

Deeply moved, this man went into his fine master bedroom, woke his wife, and told her what he had overheard. She agreed with the boy. She told him about her sons' feelings and her own, to which in his headlong rush to the top he had never given a thought.

They talked all night, and the next day he put his plans in motion. He sold his agency, bought a partnership in a small, specialized advertising business with no prospects of growing larger. With his income cut to a quarter of what it had been, he sold his house, his expensive cars, all the trappings of his former status, and settled down to enjoy his family and be a father to his boys.

He was a loving man, and he was determined. But

the first Saturday he spent with his youngest boy, doing what a ten-year-old enjoys—a baseball game, as it happened—he was horrified to find that he was bored to death and could not wait for the afternoon to end. That night at supper, while the boy was telling his brothers all about it, narrating every play of the game, every bite of popcorn and hot dog, the man could not contain himself. The tension of his effort and the heaviness of his disappointment swelled and burst within him, and he got up from the table.

The next thing he knew, he was sitting on the living-room floor, crying, with his wife and two older boys watching and his youngest boy's arms around him. "Don't worry, Daddy," the youngster was saying, "you can do it—you'll soon be one of us."

And that was the picture he drew for me, when he came to see me on an emergency appointment the next week. He was beside himself with grief. Had he made an irreparable mistake? Had he sacrificed the driving life he knew—and, let us face it, enjoyed—for a shared life with his family that was beyond his power to achieve?

It became the task of therapy to retrieve for this stricken man some part of the humanity he had lost in the years of his cold-blooded competitive struggle. Were there any toys in the attic of his mind that could be dusted off and used to humanize his relationship with his wife and sons?

Fortunately there were—a cherished telescope left from his boyhood passion for astronomy, canoe trips with companions of his youth, and a delight in wilderness camping, the camera and darkroom equipment of an amateur photographer. He had abandoned them all when he went off to college and a graduate degree in business administration, and had never looked back. Now he reclaimed them, step by step, and found that if he lacked a boy's enthusiasm, he could replace it with the larger resources of a serious adult amateur. He found points of shared interest with his boys—photography with one, astronomy with another, camping with all three and his wife as well. He began to enjoy himself, and through his children he experienced being a child again.

Unique? Or Crazy?

Few of us in the postindustrial world can find jobs that employ our individuality. More and more every day we become flattened out by a behemoth computer-culture. To assert one's own unique self involves the danger of being thought crazy. The Big Brothers of our giant institutions will do anything for us except allow us a touch of originality. A deviation from the expected is awkward, it is a foreign object in the finely meshed gears, it interrupts the smooth rhythm and may even bring the machine to a dead stop. We are graded like apples on an assembly line—out go those that won't fit exactly two dozen to the carton.

Occasionally an odd-sized apple decides to become an orange. A mother telephones me. Her voice is shrill with outrage.

"Doctor," she says, "I want you to talk to my son."

"Why should I talk to your son?" I ask.

"Something is wrong with him."

"What do you think is wrong with your dear son?"

"My son is crazy. I want you to talk——"

"Your son is crazy, you think? Well, that is not so unusual. We live in a crazy culture."

"Culture-shmulture. My son is a crazy nut."

"Well, what has this crazy nut done?"

"Doctor, he is twenty-six years old, he has a doctor's degree from the Massachusetts Institute of Technology in chemical engineering, and he is making leather belts and selling them from a hole-in-the-wall in Greenwich Village."

"So?"

"Don't you understand? He is throwing his life away. He has a doctor's degree——"

"From the Massachusetts Institute of Technology."

"Yes. He sells maybe three or four a day, some days nothing."

"You wish him to sell more than three or four?"

"Doctor, he doesn't want to work in chemical engineering. He is qualified. He could earn a good living. They need chemical engineers everywhere today. He could become a big executive and get married and buy his own home."

"Maybe he is not interested in buying his own home. . . ."

The mother was not exaggerating. The facts were as she told me, I later learned when, to please her, the young man agreed to pay me a single visit. She truly believed that her son was out of his mind. What sane person would turn down the offers four large corporations had made to her son? They pursued this virtually straight-A student right through graduate school, enticed him with an excellent starting salary, regular promotions, moving and medical expenses, insurance, expense account, help with bank loans, and at the end a fat pension to reward his lifetime of loyalty. Safely tucked in the cocoon of a research and development program, he need never have one moment of insecurity or financial need.

Short of ill health or accident, there was no way this young man could miss. The book of his life had been written, the pages numbered, the volume bound. All he had to do was follow the script as written by the biggest of Big Daddies, the multinational corporation.

Instead, not unlike Buddha who gave up wealth, opulent living, and a beautiful wife to begin a new life of asceticism and contemplation, this young man chose leather belts and Greenwich Village. As his mother perceived the situation, he had taken his highly trained brain and thrown it down the incinerator, along with the substantial investment she had made in paying for his education.

How do we estimate this young man's action? Was he risking his mother's hysteria and the scorn of a comformist society to assert a deeply felt need to be his own man, his unique human self?

Crazy he was not, only a little romantic perhaps. Since I do not play God, I made no judgments, nor did I urge him to go this way or that way. I used his visit to discuss with him the courses that were open to him and the conditions of life attached to each. He could live like an urban Saint Francis in dignified poverty, with perhaps a janitor's job to secure his livelihood. Or, having ruled out the corporate life, he could teach his specialty at a university. When he pointed out that this, too, was a compromise with values he abhorred, I willingly concurred. When I pointed out that at least he would have the option of taking a sabbatical whenever he felt the need to design leather belts in a Greenwich Village hole in the wall he also, laughing, agreed.

That was the course he finally followed after another year of bohemian experimentation. Considering that we must earn our living, and that we may as well do it with as little pain and as much time for being ourselves as we can manage, I felt that he had arranged to have the best of two possible worlds.

No Exit

And what if the road one has taken reaches a dead end and permits no return? Some people take this road blithely, confidently, never pausing to think about what its destination is likely to be. Obviously, one cannot know with any certainty. But at least one must attempt to think about what may lie ahead. There are always signs along the way.

I knew a woman who ignored all the signs for thirty-five years of her glamorous, successful life. When she started on her road to glory and financial freedom, she had not the faintest notion of who she was or what she wanted. Her mother was "too busy with men" and her grandmother raised her, filling her in childhood with fantasies of success, wealth, independence, which in fact her grandmother had never enjoyed. And so, endowed with beauty and exceptional intelligence, she plunged ahead, living the fulfillment of her grandmother's dreams.

Her rise was meteoric. She became a high-level executive in a dress-buying firm. Every year she made half a dozen trips abroad, where she was treated like a queen by the most famous couturiers in Paris, London, Rome. She earned an astronomical salary and she did not owe anything to anyone—it was all her own. She had three husbands, many lovers, and she discarded them all like empty pop bottles. She could have sex when she liked and with whom she liked. Her Park Avenue apartment was a showplace. She could go everywhere, do everything—she was free! For the time being. Not once did she stop to see where she was going.

So what happened to this vital woman, this paragon of independence?

One evening she came home to her beautiful apartment after a very successful day. She had made a real coup, a $100,000 sale to a single customer. There was nobody in her apartment to bother her or make demands on her—and nobody to greet her either, or share her satisfaction in her successful day. But that was her choice. She did not need anybody, not a husband, not an intimate friend, no close relationship of any kind. She was an independent person.

So she was sitting, having her cocktail by herself, watching the news on the television, when she happened to look down at her hand holding the glass. And idly, not thinking anything about it, she pinched the skin on the back of her hand. It did not bounce back at once, elastically, like young skin. Then she noticed that the skin was not white and smooth, as in youth, but had brown spots here and there. That was when she jumped up and went to her mirror.

It was as if she had dropped to another level of consciousness. What she saw was not the brown spots and the slightly sagging skin, but that her youth had been spent but never lived. That her single-minded drive for success had sucked up her years and they had vanished without a trace.

For three months a folly of the mind gripped her. She ran around as if on fire. She spent her days in beauty salons where they massage you and give you facials and put expensive lotions on you to make you look young. She went on slimming diets. She threw out her entire chic wardrobe and began to wear the clothes of a twenty-five year old. She took younger and younger men to expensive luncheons, basking in their flattery, even though she knew they were homosexuals and their words were mere kindness because they were not interested in her.

She neglected her work, and the inevitable happened—she was fired by her thirty-six year old boss. Of course, she arranged to lose her job. If you asked her, "Do you want to lose your job?" she would say, "Are you crazy? I love my job!" But without knowing it she *intended* this. She did what we do so often, she did what she really wanted to do, even though in her conscious mind she did not want that at all.

When she came to me she had lost too much weight, and she looked even older than her years. Her little short skirt showed cruelly the bony knees, the thin calves, and all her expensive cosmetics could not disguise the haggard face. She was very angry and she had turned her anger inward against herself, which as we know makes depression. She had all the symptoms of depression—she was not sleeping, not eating, losing weight—but she expressed only her anger.

"Can you give me back my youth?" she asked me. "Can you get me back my job? Can you get me another husband? I do not accept being old," she said furiously. "It is the end."

I said, "If it is the end, you have come to the wrong person. I am not the undertaker. And I cannot get your youth back. I am a physician, not a magician. If you have no future, I cannot help you. Why do you come to me?"

So she told me she came because she had a dream. In her dream she saw a beautiful rose lying on the ground, and she bent down to pick it up, but as she did so a hand came out of the ground and grasped her wrist and began to pull her down, down into the ground. She woke up in terror. But the dream came again and again and she was afraid to go to sleep.

What was this dream, if not a warning from that part of ourselves that we do not fool? She already knew the truth, that her life devoted to success, prestige, money was not enough, that she had missed too much, had given up too much. This was the truth that had come to her, that she could not go on living that life.

And in fact she had already attacked and destroyed it. Why had she done that? Because it was not her own, her unique life she was living, but a life of fantasy. And not even her own fantasy!

We know how often it happens to a child that a parent tries to live out his or her own fantasy through the life of the child. In this woman's case, the brilliant business career was not the idea of her mother, who was something of a tramp, nor of her father who disappeared early from her life, but of her grandmother, a woman whose actual experience of life was most limited, but who had stuffed her childhood with dreams of luxury and total independence in the great world.

It happens to many people, that they come to a point in their lives whether at fifty-five, as in this woman's case, or forty-five, even thirty-five, when they realize that they are not living their own unique, authentic life. They panic, as she did. They feel, as she felt, that they are facing catastrophe. They do not know how to make a different life. They do not even know, at this first confrontation, what is the life they in fact *intended* to live.

We are all born with a genetic endowment to make a life plan for ourselves, what in existential theory we call *intentionality*. From the day we are born, we are shaping that life plan. From our parents, our environment, our society, we take what is given us to shape that plan.

It is a secret plan. It has nothing at all to do with conscious decision, conscious choice. A conscious choice can take only a very small, narrow part of our life into consideration, only what we see and understand with our conscious mind. But this deeper plan takes all into consideration. It is made out of the whole self, the needs and demands and capabilities, the potentiality of the whole person.

Its choices are no more conscious than the choice of a child growing up in Africa to suffer sleeping sickness, or malnutrition in India, or the little girls in old China to have their feet bound. Those are accidents of the environment or the society that can change a person's life. In the same way, an accident in a child's environment anywhere can turn the child away from the intended authentic life for which that child is uniquely shaped.

An accident in our American environment, the strong influence of a father, a mother, in this case a grandmother, can turn a child aside into an inauthentic life. Many men and women pick the goals of wealth, success, prestige. And they discover, at this age or that age, that this life does not bring them the satisfactions it promised, that it does not meet their inner needs and desires.

We have other goals they might choose. Americans also try for a life of the intellect, or of adventure and novelty, or simply a life of living and loving and enjoying, making friends and close relationships, in marriage or not, having children or not, but still living like human beings. They can take time to smell a flower, eat a good meal even if not an expensive one, care about other human beings and have them care in return. This does not mean they cannot have some success and some fame as well, and even earn some wealth. But one does not have to be rich or successful to live a good life as a human being. People in all times, in all societies, have known that.

For a man or woman to come to the age of forty-five or fifty-five and discover only then that it is no longer the right life, that what seemed so good this morning is no longer good tonight—that is very hard. But it is not the end, as my patient insisted. It is a beginning. She should have been shouting hosannas at her discovery, at her new awareness. It was the beginning of a new creativity in her life.

I do not say it is easy. A therapist, of all people. knows what a difficult task it is to re-examine and re-create an entire life. If we look at ourselves often, every day a little, it is not so difficult. But if we put it off for too long, as this woman did, it is very difficult indeed.

The gravest mistake this woman made was in setting her course so narrowly that it cut her off from all relationships except functional ones. She chose to have no family, no friends, no one who might share her successes or her failures—and no one against whose values she could measure and perhaps come to question, her own. Knowing no one else, she could never know herself. And ignorance of herself led her straight to disaster.

She might have had friends and family and still

come to the edge of the cliff. Many do. Because one other quality is needed: the willingness—or perhaps the positive wish—to come to know yourself through the knowledge that you gain of others, and to examine the values by which you are living as you come to understand their values.

- *We assert our uniquesness best by recognizing that of others.*

- *The battle of the sexes stems from the blindness of men and women to each other's uniqueness.*

- *In a computerized society, just signing our names somewhere helps to prove we exist as individuals.*

- *Living someone else's life is like walking the plank; drowning is inevitable.*

- *There's a clock inside of us that contains our true intention, and when we ignore its ticking we do so at our own peril.*

- *If we look at ourselves every day a little, we can eventually see the whole person.*

The Culture Dream

8

The people who come to a therapist are usually in a state of muddle, not to say panic. They are angry, defeated, and they toss between extremes of self-justification and self-recrimination. They ask, What's wrong with me? Why do I have all this trouble in my marriage, with friends, with my job? Why am I not enjoying my life? Why can't I get it all together?

I do not speak of the profound dislocations or disorders of those whose self has gone far astray from reality. If I ask a man named Moshe Pipick, "What is your name?" and he replies, "I am Mahatma Gandhi," I can be reasonably certain that fantasy has taken over not merely a portion but the whole self.

There was a waiter in a Hungarian restaurant where I occasionally dined, who first attracted my notice by his elegant, indeed royal manner of serving a meal. When I asked him where he had learned his profession, expecting to hear that he had been trained in one of Europe's great houses, he whispered to me that he was not a waiter by trade, that he was in fact of aristocratic birth, descended from the famous Esterhazy family of Hungary. From time to time he helped out the small orchestra with his violin, and when I complimented him on his playing he took me further into his confidence. This time he was not an Esterhazy but a protegé of the great Count Esterhazy.

"Like Haydn?" I asked.

"Not *like* Haydn. . . ." and with my coffee he left me the clear implication that he *was* Haydn. His historical allusion was correct but nevertheless I arranged therapy for him with a colleague.

This raises the moral dilemma of whether one has the right to interfere in another's fantasy when that fantasy has at least the value of making bearable a life that otherwise cannot be borne. This man was still functioning in the workaday world. But there was always the danger that his delusion might take over entirely, and that he might demand the privilege of his fantasy by insisting that the Philharmonic engage him as its first violinist. Some intervention was indicated, if only to save him from arrest or at least a punch in the nose.

My waiter's fantasy was extreme. He had floated himself right off to another continent and another century as well as another personality. But he had stayed within his inherited culture. He was a Hungarian, and he had simply gone back to another Hungary, one in which he could find a princely patron for his presumably unappreciated gifts.

This is not, I find, unusual. We all daydream ourselves out of harsh reality now and then, and some who are otherwise functioning normally are in fact living their daydream. And these fantasies are not ordinarily plucked out of nowhere. They are culture-bound, tradition-bound, class-bound.

I go further. I see culture as a form of dream life into which people may either be born or may retreat for safety. The tighter it binds them, the safer they feel within the dream, the less danger there is that the cutting edge of reality will wake them.

Dreamers Here and Now

The people of Bali lived in such a culture-bound dream until the tide of Western technology washed over their island. They spent their days in a state of aesthetic intoxication, playing music, dancing, creating beautiful objects, enjoying nature and each other's humanity. Food was ample and the living was so easy that no jarring realities shook them from their culture dream. Travelers of the 1930s rightly named Bali the last paradise.

Elsewhere the culture-bound dream is likely to be of a different order and less endearing. The subculture of the lifelong gambler is bounded by the race track, the poker or crap table, the roulette wheel, the mystique of luck, and the ritualized sequence of winning and losing. Like hard-core ethnic minorities, gamblers are barely aware of a world outside their dream.

Eugene O'Neill captured such a dream-drugged culture in *The Iceman Cometh*. Through alcohol his foiled men huddled together in the comfort of their shared pipe dreams. They were threatened only if they left the barroom for the outside world where reality lurked. Were they best left inside to dream away their lives? That was the question the playwright posed.

The sweep toward a computerized society has left pockets of mini-cultures snug, sometimes smug, within a circumscribed dream life. The bank teller enacts his daily arithmetical routines, handles bundles of dream money, money that has no reality for him. He takes the five-twenty train to his house in the suburbs, enjoys a home life whose parameters have been defined by mass-culture magazines, watches dream images on television, goes to bed and dreams, no doubt about his daydream life.

Class and cultural patterns stitch us so tightly within the cloth of dreams that we are hard put to see the threads, let alone peer through them to the world beyond. A second-generation welfare recipient, hemmed within his culture of poverty, sees the world as the servant of his needs and becomes enraged when the bureaucracy does not provide the something for nothing that society owes him. A self-made man, gloating within his successful dream life, snarls at the welfare clients—they just don't *want* to work, the larcenous lazy bastards! The ethic of the worker's culture dream is incomprehensible to people whose dream lives embrace no experience of work, no tradition of a job, of money earned rather than merely received, no notion even that one has to be at a particular place at a certain time, as job-training programs repeatedly reveal.

A high-level executive takes his secretary to dinner at a very posh restaurant. They have worked late and he is giving the girl a treat in reward for her loyalty. She consults the menu, but he consults only the maître d'hôtel, and when she murmurs, "I would like the seafood," he does not even hear her. If she is bold enough to repeat her preference, he persuasively overrules her—"Oh, no, you must have the quenelles and the glazed pheasant. They do these things marvelously here."

For her the seafood—lobster, crab, oysters or whatever, all far beyond a secretary's budget—would really have been a treat. And her boss, although he really means to please her, is too encapsulated within his own cultural dream to give a thought to what would in reality give her pleasure. In his circles the man does the ordering of the dinner, come what may. And so she dutifully nibbles at quenelles and glazed pheasant, wary of these unfamiliar concoctions and regretting the oysters Rockefeller that she could have enjoyed wholeheartedly.

The truckdriver who takes the factory bookkeeper out to dinner makes very sure that she gets what she wants. He is even prepared to make a scene and send her dish back to the kitchen if she is not perfectly pleased. That is *his* version of how a man treats his woman guest.

But let's not make a culture hero of him. If he takes her to bed as the climax of the evening, he is equally capable of giving her a rough time in the event that she is not sufficiently complaisant to his wishes. *His* tradition harks back to his Polish immigrant mother who grieved that her husband no longer loved her because he no longer beat her every Saturday night.

A New York girl, acting out her culture dream of sophistication, adventure, and dangerous experimentation, marries a Texas sharecropper's son who has become a construction worker. Befogged with his *machismo*, she can see only the tip of the iceberg. Once they are married, although like her husband she works at a job all day, she finds that she is expected also to clean, shop, cook. And after dinner he sits with his beer and his newspaper while she washes the dishes alone. She takes his indifference to mean that he doesn't love her. He loves her, but in his culture a man does not do women's work. How can a fellow who teeters high on a skyscraper all day sink so low as to pick up a dishtowel?

Occasionally, a patient comes who is not enmeshed in the fantasies of his class culture or indeed of any misshapen perception of the world. Instead, he is pinioned by a dilemma between the culture pattern of his class and the opportunity for escape. He is the very antithesis of the fantasist, a cool realist who carefully figures the angles.

No Dreamer He

Such a man introduced me to his dilemma. He said, "I earn $30,000 a year and by the time I retire I will have $150,000. But I have an offer to become a bookmaker. If I last three years before I am caught, I will have $750,000. If they arrest me in two years, I will have $500,000. If I have only one year in the betting racket, I will still come out with $250,000. My trouble is that I can't decide one way or the other."

This man, a certified public accountant, did not come to me for advice on whether he should become a bookie, at the time when betting away from the race track was still against the law. He was sent by his internist because he couldn't sleep and was suffering dermatological difficulties although examination and diagnostic tests revealed nothing amiss. It took several sessions before he trusted me enough to tell me his real difficulty.

I did not tell him to stay within his culture and keep his safe CPA's $30,000 a year. I did not advise him to become a bookmaker. I am not a law enforcement officer or a spiritual adviser. I can only help people to see what their choices are.

He made his choice. He sent his wife and children to a South American city, and he went into the bookie business. He lasted three years, and when the police were looking for a betting shop to raid, his Mafia friends let them have him. So he served his six months in jail. Then he took a trip to Europe, collected his money from the Swiss bank, which incidentally had been sending regular remittances to his wife and children, and he rejoined his family in that South American city.

He had done even better than he expected. He retired from bookmaking with $980,000 capital with which to set himself up as a respected businessman and citizen in his new country. An Alec Guinness story, almost, and without the handcuffs at the end.

How easy, how tempting it might have been for a man in his situation to have returned to the gambling community after his jail term and dreamed away the rest of his life! I do not claim that therapy kept him coolly away from the gambling culture. But it kept him from agonizing over alternatives, and it kept his body from breaking out into any more angry hives.

Patient Griselda

Every one of us is caught in the dream of his sub-culture to some degree. The filaments woven by parents, teachers, peers, the repeated shibboleths, and the dramatized culture patterns of the mass media all ensnare us. We become enmeshed. And many remain comfortable in the cozy blanket of conformity.

A vast majority of the human race are at ease only in the tradition in which they are reared, and change to them is a major disaster. To others the culture dream may be crippling, and only some extricating event or personal crisis sets them free to pursue their selfhood. Freedom sometimes comes dramatically, as it did to one patient of mine, a good old-fashioned wife who seemed to be living in another century.

She had been a shy, rather plain girl in her youth, without much education or drive to earn her own living. Marriage was her only hope and she had little confidence in her chances of getting a husband. When a suitor finally came and she was about to be married, her mother earnestly advised her.

"Take care of your husband," her mother said. "Cook

for him what he likes. Keep the house nice for him. Give him sex whenever he wants. Look after him, and he will look after you, so that in sickness and in old age you will never have to worry."

She lived by this maternal rule for twenty-five years, obeying it to the letter. Her children grew up and left home. And then came catastrophe.

When she came to me she was still in her forties, not an old woman by any standard. But she came in a wheelchair, pushed by her husband, and she looked haggard and old. She was suffering from a pain in her leg that was so relentless, so intractable, that she was not aware of her surroundings, did not even look up and answer when I greeted her.

She had been to many doctors, had undergone every relevant test, and the doctors had found nothing to account for her pain. There was a negligible arthritis in the spine, a slight inflammation of the sciatic nerve, but nothing that would not normally be relieved by a few aspirins now and then. Yet, she was not only unable to walk—she could not sleep, could not eat, could not attend to what was said to her. She had been sent to me as a last resort before undergoing nerve surgery that might relieve her pain but would leave her little better than a vegetable for what remained of her life.

They were barely inside the door when her husband blurted out, "This is the last—after this I am through! I have taken her to doctor after doctor, but she is too sick, I have no more patience with this. I wouldn't watch a dog suffer like this."

His overbearing, bullying tone offended me and I said, mildly enough, "But she is not a dog, she is your wife." When he answered in the same offensive way I said, half-joking, "You are a sourpuss! To live with a man like you could give anyone a pain!"

I glanced at the woman and saw that she had raised her head—she was actually listening. So I took a chance and went on to deliver a lecture on human compassion and empathy for another's suffering. I said, "It would not surprise me to discover that you are your wife's pain. It just might be that your attitude toward her is the cause of your wife's affliction."

"Yes!" his wife suddenly exclaimed. "Yes, yes, yes!" She was sitting forward in her wheelchair and her face had come to life. So I continued, expanding on the theme of how one person can cripple another one, emotionally and even physically, by treating the other as a function, a mechanical convenience, never as a human being.

I did not say that, of course, the other also contributes by submissively accepting this treatment— she was not ready for that. Her husband spluttered but I did not let him speak. She was nodding at my every word, offering now and then a confirming comment of her own. About half an hour went by, and then her voice suddenly rang out.

"Doctor, I have no pain!" she cried. "For the first time in seven months I have no pain!"

That was only the beginning of her cure; an illness that had developed over twenty-odd years could not be dissipated in twenty-odd minutes. Weeks of therapeutic sessions went by before she remembered some crucial details about the onset of her pain. She had had an argument with her husband, the first time she had opposed him in all the years of their marriage, and he had taunted her with the boast that he did not have to put up with her, that he could get himself a nice young wife just by lifting a finger. She was too shocked to answer, but she experienced a fierce impulse to kick him in the groin—a violence totally uncharacteristic of her—and she had suppressed it.

That night she dreamed that she was in an accident and lost her left leg. Her mother came to her in the dream, saying, "You see? I told you to be careful. . . ." She awoke in terror and tried to sit up, but she found that she could not, because her left leg was in dreadful pain.

So what shall we say of this excessively good wife? Clearly she was the captive of a cultural fantasy, that a good wife was a submissive and selfless wife, and she was unfortunate in having married a man who took full advantage of her submissiveness, degrading her to the level of a doormat. She had accepted her mother's outworn precept, never questioning it until her repressed psyche had done violence to her body.

A doormat does not rise up and aim a kick at the man who is wiping his shoes on it!

The cultural stereotype in which this woman found herself might be called the Jewish-mother syndrome, although it is not necessarily Jewish or motherly or even female. Men have also been afflicted by the compulsion to be all-enduring, all-forgiving victims.

A Jewish-mother story to end them all may be this one, which came out of the Russian ghetto of the last century, the story of a Jewish lad who fell in love with a Gentile girl. The girl held back, and finally to discourage him she told him that she would marry him if he proved his love by killing his mother and bringing her the mother's beating heart. The youth shuddered, begged her to reconsider, but when she was adamant he nerved himself to the deed. He killed his mother, tore out her heart, and ran with it still beating to his beloved. On the way he stumbled and fell. "Oh, my poor boy, I hope you didn't hurt yourself!" exclaimed the Jewish mother's heart.

The Genetic Factor

Obviously, cultural forces do not work alone. Nor are they necessarily malevolent, waiting to entrap the weak and the unwary, as with the doormat wife. Cultural factors and genetic factors can work in benign collusion to bring about beautiful people, gifted people, the brave as well as the cruel.

Every human being is born at the end of a long chain of life reaching back millions of years to the first homo sapiens. His genetic code, his accidental share of his ancestors' genes, has been drawn by the lottery of successive generations from that enormous gene pool. By themselves, except for chance mutations, the genes are immutable. But when worked upon by environmental forces they are activated, brought into play. All aspects of an environment—mother, father, siblings, economic and educational influences, geography, the historal epoch into which a child is born—play a part in potentiating the genes. And no single environment, with all its aspects, can activate all of an individual's inherited capabilities.

The same child born into a different cultural setting would be a totally different person. He might well look the same, for the genetic code has already determined how tall, how fat, how nimble, how fair or dark he will be. But even these genetic factors are modified by environmental factors such as poor nutrition or endemic disease. A person could be endowed with great physical strength or harmonious features or a long life span, but these are all potential and an unfavorable culture can rob him even of these genetic gifts.

A case in point was a tall, skinny youth who regularly made deliveries to me and was always whistling some tune, always a different one and never one I could recognize. Once I asked him to identify a tune that was singularly haunting. He looked amazed that I should be at all interested.

"It's no song—nobody wrote it," he said, "it's just a tune, my own tune. I made it up."

I took out my guitar and played it, and the boy was delighted. I told him that I had a musician friend who could write out the notes of his tunes, and might even teach him a little notation so that he could write them down himself. He looked at me with astonishment and joy.

I was curious to know what his parents thought of his habit of making up tunes. He said, "My father thinks I'm nutty and my brothers kid me about it." This was no surprise. His family lived in the notorious slum of Hell's Kitchen, and his father and five brothers —he was the youngest—were big burly longshoremen. They made fun of him because he was skinny and underdeveloped, and his brothers called him a sissy because he did not like fighting or working on the docks.

The family had sent him out to work at sixteen, after two years of high school. Without the accident of meeting someone who took an interest in his musical aptitude, this boy might have gone from messenger to stock clerk, perhaps to end up as the head of a mail room in some office. Instead, with the help of my musician friend, he developed his musical gift, a gift that came to him through the genetic game of roulette. He eventually became a successful songwriter and the pride of his family and, because he was a good son, he set his mother up in a house in the country.

Genetic transmission is full of mystery. There was no history of a musician in that family. But poor families do not know much of their history, and if indeed there was a musical gift in an earlier generation, perhaps there too the cultural climate was not the kind to nurture the seed of talent.

Another instance of a gift that might have been not merely wasted but a handicap is that of an incorrigible boy who was brought to the clinic where I was in service. His mother complained, "He has the devil in him! He can read our minds—he knows what we're going to do before we do it!"

The mother's intelligence was below average but her boy's was at the genius level, his IQ well above 160. This child's future lay in the balance, for in his environment he might readily have developed into a sociopathic personality. In his family's tight little culture, there was no place for a child of such superior intelligence.

Instead it was arranged to place him in a doctor's family, and with proper education and guidance he became a physician, able to lead a fruitful life that made full use of his gifts. Thus, an act of chance, or the work of therapy, can snatch a person from a path that would otherwise lead only to a dead end, if not worse.

Cinderella's Escape

We come to understand many puzzling aspects of people when we see their culture or subculture as a consciously experienced daydream, in which they may float more or less contentedly but which renders them directionless, selfless, prisoners of the dream. As they grow older, some are able to break out of their fantasies by themselves, and escape to regain a part of their individuality. Others crumble when their dream is dashed against some obtruding reality. Such people suffer not from neurosis but from a superimposed set of rules and values derived from their cultural background, which they have never questioned. It is not often easy to see the difference between a neurotic problem and a problem that stems from the discrepancy between the culture dream and the existential reality.

Responsible therapy tries to help dissipate the dream sooner rather than later in life, to peel away the culture layer by layer. Some are able to escape the cultural dream before serious discontent or a crisis of the personality occurs.

I remember a beautiful girl from my early days of

service in the hospital clinic. She was a black-haired, blue-eyed Irish beauty, but her lovely face was marred by a most unlovely rash. The dermatologist found no medical explanation for the skin eruption and so he passed her on to me for a psychological examination, in search of a possible psychosomatic origin.

The family history soon gave me a clue. There were three daughters of this closely knit Irish family. The eldest—"She's the religious one. She went into the convent." The second sister—"She's the beauty of the family. She's got herself a very nice husband and they have their first child." And my patient, this pretty girl with the ugly blotches on her face?

"Oh, I was to stay at home. I'm not religious enough to be a nun, and I was too plain to get a husband. . . ."

So the family had told her, since she was a little girl. And she accepted the plainness and the lack of religious fervor. But she was too spirited to stay at home. Against her parents' wish she had taken a business course after graduation from the nuns' school, and got herself a job as a typist. And then, to her astonishment, she had met a young man who did not think she was so plain and wanted to marry her. He was a good young man, who had a job as a salesman and was studying accounting in night school so that he could one day hope to support a family.

And now, just as she was going to have her happiness at last, here was this terrible rash.

What did her family say to all this? She sighed. Her father had not spoken to her since the day she got a job. Her mother told her the rash was God's punishment because she had not obeyed her parents and stayed at home to look after them in their old age. And she almost believed it, except that her fiancé laughed at her and told her it was just nervousness because their wedding day was only a few weeks off, and to go and get something for the rash from the doctors at the clinic and everything would be all right. So she had come to the clinic. . . .

Well, of course, we cleared up the rash and we talked out the blend of guilt and anxiety that was behind it, and Cinderella escaped from the cinders and married her good young man. The rash no doubt would break out again from time to time, because there is no absolute antidote to the teaching instilled in childhood, but she would not be upset by it and it would go away.

We need our struggles for identity and independence. We need traditions and rules, and we even need cultural bonds. But we need to recognize them as bonds, to press against them and to shake ourselves free of them when the time comes to escape. The bonds are a welcome shield to those who have no wish to escape. And those who want to break the bonds can usually find the way, if they want to badly enough. If they are also aware of what they are escaping from, and why, then they are on the way to the existential road.

This liberation does not come unsought. It comes only to those who reach out to others. Others may have a different cultural heritage, or they may be suffering the same constrictions that we suffer, but seeing them in others, we recognize them in ourselves.

Many young people who flee their small towns for the wider experience of the metropolis have made that discovery. They have seen their cultural patterns in parents and siblings, and have broken free—but only because others have shown them, knowingly or not, their bonds.

What they do in the new and more diverse setting is, of course, another matter. They may carry their old culture patterns with them, for better or worse; a mere change of wallpaper does not change the self. But at least in the new environment they come to know others of more varied backgrounds, and seeing themselves over and against these others they can discover what to discard, and perhaps what also to keep, of their inherited ways and values.

- *What a pity it is to be so locked within one's own dream as never to share the dream of another.*

- *The security blanket of conformity is warm and*

comfortable—just so it doesn't cover our heads and smother us.

- *Blind luck can make a genius; to be decent, human, and caring takes more.*

- *To escape from your background is no great achievement, unless you know what you are escaping into.*

The Art of Renegotiation

9

The woman sat down in my office, sighed, and said, "Doctor, I have been married for twenty-six years. My husband is a dear good man. He would give me the moon if I wanted it. He still courts me like Romeo courting Juliet."

I said, "But that is charming! You are a fortunate woman."

She laughed, and then she began to cry. "Doctor, look at me!" she said. "I'm forty-nine, overweight, wrinkled. I am a mother of grown children. Do I look like a Juliet? Can I feel like a Juliet? How would you like to play the balcony scene every night for twenty-six years? But he expects it. He would be heartbroken if I didn't go along with it. I can't bear to hurt him. But I can't go on any longer—I'm a tired old woman! Doctor, what am I going to do?"

She was right—it was both a laughing and a crying matter. The scene she drew was ludicrous, and it was also sad. Even Juliet, if she had lived to bear children and reach the age of forty-nine, would find life with the Romeo of the balcony scene a little bit wearing, would find it hard to respond to protestations of passion with a middle-aged paunch.

Obviously this real-life Juliet was entitled to a new marriage contract, in which acting out her husband's over-age fantasy was no longer a part.

All our contracts with each other—marriages, friendships, parent-child relationships—must be renegotiated from time to time. Circumstances change. People change. Old bonds wither. New needs arise and demand to be met.

Secret Contracts

All relationships are contracts, whether spoken or unspoken, and of course for generations every marriage was not only a spoken but a written contract. In Europe this is still so to some extent. Property changed hands, dower rights were specified, and even the portions of children not yet conceived were precisely stated. The marriage contract was a legal instrument and both parties knew exactly where they stood.

As for their personal relationship with each other, that too was a contract supported by society, family, church. The marriage was sustained, happy or not. Discontented husbands and wives found other sources of comfort. The mistress and the lover were accepted conventions in the European upper classes, provided the affair was pursued discreetly and the proprieties were preserved intact. An Emma Bovary who threw all discretion out of the carriage window was rare enough to be a worthy subject for Flaubert's great novel, and her end, inevitably, was tragic.

More recently, and especially in this country, the written marriage contract has fallen into contempt. Marriage was not for property or security, it was for love. Yet, even this romantic approach implied a contract. Each party had expectations, indeed demands, that the marriage was to fulfill. The difference was that these demands were not written down in a legal instrument, were often not even discussed. The lovers themselves were too frequently unaware of these secret clauses in the unwritten agreement. Their unconscious demands on each other became conscious only when the demands went unmet. And unmet demands, when they surface, are usually unreasonable, outrageous, fueled by months and years of stored resentment.

The consequences of these secret contracts appear in the divorce courts, where one out of three marriages—in California, one out of two—come to an end. For a long time a significant peak in the divorce rate appeared in the twentieth year of marriage. Whole generations of men and women reached the breaking point after sharing nearly half their adult lives. What had brought them to this point?

A Short Story

Many of them have passed through my consulting room on the way to the divorce court. I remember one that might have served a writer other than Flaubert, perhaps an O. Henry, if not for a novel then at least for a short story.

It was the husband who came to see me. He had been married for nineteen and a half years. One evening he came home a little later than usual, just at dinner time, and as he walked into the apartment his wife greeted him with the question, "Where were you?"

He answered pleasantly that he had been with some friends. His wife persisted. "What friends? Whom did you see? Where did you go?"

He made various evasive answers, but she carried on the catechism through the cocktails, the roast, the dessert, becoming more aggressive with each course, until he threw down his napkin and stood up.

"What right have you to ask me these questions?" he demanded. "I've told you I was with friends—isn't that enough?"

"No, it isn't enough!" she answered. "As your wife I have the right to know everything! A marriage is nothing if it isn't based on complete candor between husband and wife!"

"But haven't I the right to at least a little privacy, a few secrets?"

"There can be no secrets between husband and wife!"

"Now you are exercising thought control!"

"A husband and wife must know *everything* about each other——"

"I never understood that to be the terms of our marriage," he answered, and he got his coat and left the house.

This man had no wish to destroy what had been a comfortable, stable relationship, and he was appalled by the painful disruptions, not to mention the expenses, that he could expect with a divorce. But what had begun as a trivial quarrel ended by turning up a host of previously unuttered, fiercely hostile discontents, and divorce was the outcome.

Where had he been, in fact, that afternoon? He told me what he had refused to tell his wife. He had been buying her a birthday present.

The Singer and the Male Chauvinist Husband

And here is another case of an unwritten, unspoken contract. This time it was the wife who told the story.

"My husband said to me, 'You'll never be a singer! Give up these choirs and choruses, they'll never get you anywhere. Get yourself a job, teach singing instead of running off on these oratorio dates, so that at least you can stay home and take care of the house and the children!'"

A male chauvinist pig, right? Plainly, as she told me, he was trying to destroy her as a human being. Why must she give up her hope of being discovered by some concert manager, her ambition of becoming a concert artist, and be nothing more than a housewife for the rest of her life?

But what about him, and what about the children? This husband was a hard-working dentist, and he would come home and find a note on the refrigerator. His wife was off to Utah to sing in a cantata, he was to call for the children at the neighbor's apartment, there was this and this in the refrigerator that he was to cook for supper.

There is nothing wrong with having hopes and ambitions. But this woman was married, with a husband and children, and yet she went on living like a single woman, without any responsibility except to her own hopes and ambitions. She had entered into a contract to be a wife and mother—but she had entered it with her fingers crossed, like a child who is telling a lie. The crossed fingers stood for a secret clause that negated the entire contract, the clause saying that she was still free to abandon husband and children at a moment's notice or none at all, and pursue her dream of becoming a concert artist.

Of course, her husband was also at fault for letting matters come to the breaking point. He loved his beautiful, talented, youthful wife, who at thirty-nine still looked like nineteen. The trouble was that she still behaved like nineteen, still lived on the hope of a concert career that was born in her when she won a prize for singing while she was still in high school. He had taken pride in her singing, had done what he could to nurture her career long after the hope of her becoming a concert artist was realistic.

So at thirty-nine she made the choice she should have made many years earlier between her dream of a singing career and her reality as a wife and mother. She got a divorce. Her husband had a hard time—it is not easy to find a mother substitute—but he found a divorced woman with two children of her own and they pooled their families and their needs.

This marriage was a clear contract with all its terms understood. His new wife would go on with her profession as a clinical psychologist, and he would go on with his as a dentist. They made their financial and household arrangements for two working parents and four children, not on the basis of love and romance, or even primarily of sex, but on the foundation of the actual needs of six living human beings.

And what of the charming, childlike singer? Out in the real world, alone and unsupported, she soon discovered the hollowness of the dream for which she had given up her home, her children, and a husband who had truly cared for her. In the end she followed the course she had so bitterly scorned when he suggested it. She became a singing teacher, and an excellent one, who brought to her pupils' problems the wisdom she had gained too late for herself.

Dreams, Unlimited

A good-looking young Italian came to see me, in a state of rage that had gone beyond his control. He was afraid he was homicidal, or suicidal, all because the dream clause in his marriage contract had been canceled. Naturally, it had been a private clause shared with no one, not with his bride and certainly not with her parents, who had dictated all the other clauses.

He said, "Doctor, the only reason I married her was to get into her father's business. I wanted a big desk with buttons to push and beautiful secretaries rushing in, I wanted a white Mercedes with a built-in bar and a telephone. What's wrong with wanting?"

He had grown up in a slum neighborhood, a bright boy with no resources except a small musical talent, and he became a musician in one of the little Greenwich Village night clubs. There he met a nice Jewish girl with a rich father, and he saw his future opening up before him, a vision of everything he yearned for. He made love to her the way Italians do—"You are an angel, you are my madonna. . . ." So her parents said, "If he loves you so much, let him prove it. We are good orthodox Jews. Let him become a Jew."

He was willing. He learned all the 633 rules of being a good orthodox Jew and he had himself ritually circumcised, fulfilling his rather painful part of the agreement. His prospective father-in-law, observing the unspoken convention in these circumstances, took him into the business.

And so they were married, and he had his big desk with the buttons and the secretaries, the white Mercedes with the bar and the telephone. And soon after the wedding his father-in-law died, the surviving partners did not want the son-in-law, and job, dream, and marriage collapsed together.

His rage when he came to me was all against his wife. Why was he angry with her, so angry that he felt he might kill her? "But if I can't be angry with her, then I have to be angry with myself. And why am I to blame?"

What was to blame was not himself but his private dream clause. Whether his marriage could have survived even with the realization of his dream must be anybody's guess. Without the dream it was doomed. He and his wife parted, and he went back to his Italian neighborhood and his night-club musician's world.

But he was, as I said, not stupid, and he had learned something from his brief expedition into Jewish big business. He organized a booking agency for night-club performers, small but it made him a living. And so he had a desk, although without the buttons and the secretaries, and a car, although not a Mercedes.

What's wrong with wanting, as this young man asked, or for that matter with dreaming? There's nothing wrong, surely. We need our fantasies and our dreams. But to build a marriage on a dream is to invite disaster, even when the dream is not secret but shared.

A shared dream brought disaster to a couple who came to see me because the husband was in a deep, perhaps a dangerous depression. They had lived their whole marriage, some fifteen years, with the dream of a house that they would own one day, a beautiful, spacious house with grounds where they would have flower gardens, a vegetable garden, fruit trees. It would be, to set a price on it, a $150,000 house.

They had been dreaming for fifteen years when city apartment rents began to soar, and they decided that they should be putting their money into owning instead of renting. It was time to buy their dream house.

But when they sat down with paper and a sharp pencil, the dream shattered. Using all their savings, mortgaging their entire future, they still could not muster enough capital for more than, at best, a $40,000 property.

To the husband this was a mortal blow. He fell into such depths of despair that his wife became worried, and so we sat in my office and talked it over.

I said, "But what is so terrible? You can escape this rent-gouging city and have your own house, a nice little house, with a little space for flowers and tomatoes, maybe, and a couple of trees. What if it is smaller than you hoped? You can live delightfully in a $40,000 house!"

The husband moaned, "I don't want a $40,000 house. I want my beautiful house, my dream house. I don't want to live if I can't live in my dream house. . . ." And his wife looked at me with big, frightened eyes.

It was sad and it was absurd. These two people could never have bought the house of their dreams. He had never earned more than $19,000 a year as a furniture salesman and she was stuck at $12,000 as bookkeeper in a small company. He was ready to die over a house that had never existed, that they could never have had. He had come face to face with the truth, not only that he could never have his house but that he could not even dream of it any more.

In the end this insubstantial dream was itself expensive. It cost these two not only pain and suffering, but the fee for a course of therapy that brought the husband out of his depression, and gave him the strength to accept what was not, after all, such a bad existential reality.

Marriage Contracts, New Style

Not long ago I was asked to speculate on what might be a marriage contract for today. Young couples about to marry, when they went to a physician for their Wassermann tests, would incidentally have a medical checkup, and in the old days they would expect to be given some instructions on sex.

A premarital sexual consultation would be laughable for the young sophisticates of today. But suppose a pair of lovers, about to marry and earnestly intending to make a good life together, came to me for a premarital psychological consultation. What would I say to them?

The marriage contract is, of course, back in fashion, in a somewhat new form. Women's liberationists quite rightly urge that all financial arrangements and each party's rights and duties be clearly understood—who cleans, who shops, who cooks, whether and when to have children and how the child care is to be divided. Questions of leisure time, of pursuing separate interests and friendships, of fidelity versus sexual freedom —these are also part of the modern marriage contract if it is openly and honestly made.

All these questions come down to one question. How

open and honest can they in fact be? It is the same with the practical matters of money and management as with the more intimate ones. All are emotionally tinged, and a disagreement about washing the dishes can be as destructive as one about having a sexual fling with the spouse's best friend.

So my advice to them would be, on the surface, simple and brief. I would say, "Make your contract. Discuss it as thoroughly as you would if it were a business deal, an employment contract, the purchase of an apartment or a house. Examine your feelings about every point at issue, and if there is disagreement, have it out now rather than later. Most important of all, don't bring to the discussion only your intellectual self, or your ideological self, or your romantic self, or your wishful, fantasizing self. Bring your true self."

And already it is not so simple. What is the true self?

Surely we can assume that our young pair are neither novices at sex nor strangers to each other. They are undoubtedly lovers and they may already have been living together, sharing the household, the finances, the working and social life that they will continue to share after they marry. Presumably they know each other and presumably they also know themselves.

But do they? How many layers of the self have they indeed penetrated? How many wishes, fantasies, dreams, and unrealistic expectations do they unconsciously see fulfilled in each other?

So I add a caution to my advice. I say, "Beware of overexpectation. Allow for each other's growth and change. Rejoice in each other, but remember that there is a serpent in every Eden and yours is not likely to be an exception. Don't wait until discontent grows from a worm into a dragon breathing fire and smoke. When the little worm lifts its head in the garden, that's the time to renegotiate."

Even as I say this, I sigh. Where is the poetry, the mystery, the romance in such a contractual marriage? But the sigh is pure nostalgia, pure sentimentality. Who wants mysteries, when one may someday open the locked door and find a witch or a Bluebeard lurking behind it?

Love on the Wing

One couple that I know have the most remarkable contractual history in all my experience. They were married years ago, when the old form of marriage agreement was past and the new one was not yet thought of. But they had a peculiar situation and they dealt with it at the outset. The husband was a salesman of highly specialized technical equipment, and his job required him to travel to the four corners of the earth. He was away at least eighteen or twenty days out of every month.

So they agreed that when they were apart, each of

them should have complete freedom, socially and sexually. But when they were together, none of their separate involvements should be allowed to interfere, not in action, thought, or even by allusion, in their companionship with each other.

It worked splendidly for a while. The husband's homecomings were celebrations. The wife had the house sparkling, cooked all his favorite dishes, and they enjoyed each other without reservation. But then on one of his visits home he contracted gonorrhea. He had been in South America, Hawaii, the Pacific, Southeast Asia, the Middle East, but he had to come home to get the clap—from his wife, who had been infected by the gentleman in the next apartment.

Well, it isn't such a serious matter any more, and it was quickly diagnosed and cured. But he had a little bad luck with it. He developed a prostatitis, and as a result he was left with a contraction of the urethra so that every time he urinated he was painfully reminded of his wife's extramarital life at home.

Wisely, he did not brood on it, but brought the matter up for discussion on his next return home. She was entirely sympathetic, and they renegotiated the sexual freedom clause in their agreement. From then on they would both observe a rule of fidelity.

She did try. But when he was away she was genuinely lonely, and she found it hard to sleep alone, night after night. She also discovered what every woman living alone discovers, that she was fair game for every man whose invitation to dinner, to the theater, to a concert, she accepted. If she clung to her chastity she was welcome to do so, but she would do it alone. She would have no companionship at all. So she slipped once, then more than once, and soon she was back in her original pattern of sexual adventure during her husband's absence.

She felt it was unfair to hold him to his promise when she had broken hers, so again they renegotiated. This time they switched roles. He had an opportunity to change from a traveling to an administrative job in his company, and he volunteered to take over the home-keeping and child care if she wanted to travel. For her the change was welcome. She got herself a selling job with an international cosmetics firm, and off she went.

At first both were content. He was a loving father and he enjoyed the new relationship with his children. He even became a good cook, and the traveler's home-coming again became a celebration. But meanwhile the children were growing up, spending less and less time with him, and after a time he became restless. Finally, when the second child went off to college and only one, a boy of sixteen, was left at home, he put a third proposal to his wife.

"Let's put Dickie in boarding school, and we'll both travel," said he. "Fine!" said she.

And that is how it has been ever since. But with both traveling it has been almost impossible to arrange their schedules so that they can spend any time at home together. He gets in on a Tuesday, they have an evening and a night, and on the Wednesday morning she flies off on her next trip. Their lovemaking became a race between consummation and a dash to the airport, and with their infrequent meetings it dwindled away altogether.

The last time I heard from them they were both still on the wing. They call themselves married friends now, because although they still have a warm and dependable attachment, they share almost nothing of their lives any more except their interest in their children. The apartment is still there for each to come home to, but they are almost never there together. An odd marriage, but they are both people who enjoy change, excitement, new scenes, new people. And so it suits them.

But I would not recommend an air-borne marriage to everyone!

Ludwig Beethoven, Marriage-Wrecker

Lives change, people change, and even the best marriage contract cannot meet all future developments. The wife who came to me had entered into marriage twelve years before with good sense and reasonable expectations.

She and her husband were both high school teachers,

he in mathematics, she in music. She had gone on with her studies after marriage and earned her doctorate in musicology, and she was now a Beethoven specialist and an assistant professor in college. Her husband, an easygoing man, had remained where he was, a high school teacher.

She said, "Doctor, he bores me! We have nothing in common, nothing at all. Even having sex with him is boring to me now."

I thought of marriages I had seen in my own generation and medical profession, of women who had married young, while their husbands were still students, and who had worked and sacrificed to put their husbands through medical school, through internships and residencies and the struggle of beginning a practice—only to find that their husbands had risen to a social level beyond them and no longer wanted to continue the marriage. So now the shoe is on the other foot, although today neither husbands nor wives are so willing to make the sacrifices they made in the past. This wife had paid her own way, but still she owed her husband some human consideration, and she acknowledged it.

"Surely there are things you still enjoy doing together in your leisure time? Pleasures you share, friends of the past?"

She shook her head. "He goes to football games and watches television. Our old friends are no longer interesting to me. I have a whole circle of new friends now, college faculty friends, musician friends. I go to concerts with them, play music with them. Music is my whole life, and my husband has no interest in sharing it."

That cut both ways. If he was not interested in sharing her life, neither was she interested in sharing his. And it seemed to me that she was making little enough effort to take him along into her new world, indeed that she was rather pointedly shutting him out of it. She had become a music snob.

But there it was, the existential reality. She had come to consult me, but that was no more than a sop to her conscience. It takes two to save a marriage, and the Beethoven lady did not really want to save hers.

If the will is there, if each partner has some awareness of, some feeling for the other as a unique human being, then something can be done. A human being is not just a high school teacher or a music scholar. A human being is a unique complexity with many facets, and somewhere a facet of one human being can be found to complement a facet of the other. If this Beethoven lady and her husband both wanted to preserve their marriage, and were willing to explore themselves and each other to find the matching facets, then they might very well be able to achieve a successful renegotiation.

Two people can make a marriage on the slenderest of links. We all know couples who are indissolubly bound to each other by nothing but their mutual aggression. They fight and make love, fight and make love. Even if they divorce they still fight—over money, custody, whatever pretext—and sometimes, even though one or both may have married again, they even come together and make love.

Shared work, a business or profession pursued together, is a bond. So is shared play. Some couples stay together only for the skiing, the tennis, the bridge.

I know one couple who stay together only to eat.

That is not a joke, it is a fact. They are both passionate about French food, and it is astonishing how much time and interest one can invest in such a passion. They dine out together in French restaurants, comb the city to discover new ones and try them out, hold long discussions with headwaiters and chefs. They collect cookbooks and recipes, share their palatal ecstasies with friends, spend hours together in their kitchen preparing new dishes. As long as their gourmet pleasures endure, their marriage will endure.

And is that necessarily a poor basis for a marriage? Marriages may be made in heaven, but it is perhaps too much to ask that they be heaven on earth. A marriage can be good even if it is not all things to each partner. A marriage is, if nothing more, at least a convenience and a comfort. And if it can also be a companionship, even a limited companionship, that is an added value in the quality of life.

The one caution is that the terms of the companionship be understood, that neither partner demands more than the partnership can provide—and that both care enough to develop the art of renegotiation. It is the disappointed secret dreams, the unspoken fantasies and unuttered expectations, that bring bitterness and hostility where once there was love.

It matters little on what grounds we meet, whether as lovers, friends, siblings, colleagues, as long as we meet in a mutual effort at openness and honesty. And if we do not know enough about ourselves at first to achieve that openness, we soon learn. By confrontation with each other, we soon discover what is important to us and what is unimportant, what we can yield to accommodate the other and where we must stand firm in defense of our different need. And so, without hostility, without resentment, with full acceptance of the other's differences as well as our own, we negotiate.

The art of renegotiation is not only the art of maintaining our links with one another. It may turn out to be the art of living to our own fullest capacity as individuals.

- *Every relationship is a contract, and it is wise to know the terms.*

- *It is beautiful to take each other on trust—until we discover the secret clause.*

- *If the will is there, anything can be the basis of a relationship.*

- *We can give up much to keep a lover or a friend—
  but only by honest negotiation.*

- *A good contract is one in which you give up
  what you can comfortably spare.*

- *If all couples were to know in advance the precise
  terms of their marriage, the institution of marriage
  might yet become the wave of the future.*

Free to Be Good or Bad

10

Now to the final question.

What can we do to be free, to live humanly yet with self-interest?

It is essential that we first take a long, hard look at what our beliefs are as to good and bad. For many of our beliefs are unavoidably encumbered by the mythologies of past generations, and sometimes they include those of hucksters who have sold us their self-improvement panaceas.

We all know there is evil in the world. Good and

evil have been man's obsession since the Garden. We know there are frauds and larcenists. We also know there are tigers and poisonous snakes and predators that are only fulfilling their natures. But man is not a tiger or a poisonous snake, and when he behaves like one he cannot be viewed in human terms.

Our concern is of a different magnitude. We are seeking to redefine our humanity, to see it anew as if for the first time. We need, all of us, to cleanse our minds of encrusted attitudes that say that good is inevitably pure while bad is corrupt and never the twain shall mix.

We can ask ourselves questions, plucked out of daily life:

Are we "good" when we devote ourselves to the care of an aging parent, "bad" when we refuse?

How much of a grown child's demands should a parent yield to in order to be a "good" mother or father?

What accommodation is each of us going to make toward a "good" marriage, and at what cost?

Are there limits to the demands a friend, spouse, or lover can expect you to meet, in order for you to be judged a "good" person?

Do we unconsciously envision some heavenly reward for being "good," or hellfire for being "bad"?

What of the emotionally dependent widow who pressures her bachelor son to move in with her and assuage her loneliness? Is he a cold-hearted, selfish, "bad" son if he firmly rejects her pleas in defense of his own social and sexual needs?

The answers to such questions become obvious if we remember that none of the choices we make or the decisions we take is pure. Each is weighted with ego needs and considerations of self. If, in our own minds, all our actions were as pure as the driven snow, unmixed with self-interest, then indeed one would be justified in suggesting that we have our heads examined.

Because a rigid—yes, idealistic belief that human behavior comes in a bottle, labeled either good or bad, is a prescription for disillusionment and confusions of the mind.

When such rigidity occurs in institutions, the consequences are even more drastic. Did not the Inquisitors burn Joan at the stake on the principle that theirs was the only good? Remember when a whole society condemned Galileo as a bad guy? And believed Nixon a good guy?

Consider the powerful, domineering father who is convinced that his truth is everybody's truth. He raises his only son in the iron-bound Puritan tradition that unrelenting work is the only goal of man, and success its only worthy reward. The son is taught that work must come first—pleasure is for later. But for this son, pleasure never did come. By the time success came, he was sexually impotent with his beautiful and loving wife, until in desperation he abandoned her, threw up his career, and for five years, until he sought my help, remained a wrecked and pathetic recluse.

Did not this father wish only "good" for his son? Of course. But his perception of good was viewed through the lens of his own compulsions, and tragedy was the result.

In our haste to rubber-stamp human behavior either good or bad, we miss the target everyone wants to hit: to gain the insight that will help us to make our soundest choices, and to live with them comfortably, if not ecstatically.

Yet, people miss the target so often! Why? Consider the mental phenomenon of the "hidden agenda."

A young woman admires a young man very much and decides to marry him. What she says—and believes—she admires are his decent character, his excellent manners, his good looks. But she also speculates, in the privacy of her secret thoughts, that he is potentially a "money-maker," that one day he will become rich and she will live luxuriously. This expectation she tucks away in a place where she cannot find it, because it is mercenary—and therefore not "good"—to marry in the hope of riches. It is more respectable to marry a man for his decent character. Result: He does not turn out to be a money-maker and she doesn't get a life of luxury. Her secret hope, her hidden agenda, rises out of its hiding place to nag her. She becomes disappointed and bitter, deserts her husband for being too dull or for any rationalization that springs to her confused mind.

So often our choices meet defeat because they were made on the hidden agenda, which is usually based not on realistic expectation but on wishful fantasy. And, as we know only too well and after it is too late, choices made on wishes are made blindly and without considering the realistically possible outcome.

The soldier who deserts and flees to a foreign land is embittered because he is not allowed to return to his own country without suffering punishment. His desertion may have been on the highest principles, but he did not consider the cost of adhering to principle; people throughout history have paid for their principles with their lives. In making his choice he short-circuited any rational consideration of the consequences, and in his enforced exile he stews in the juices of anger and injustice.

A man pulls a knife and kills his attacker on a ghetto street. His defenders blame his act on "society," which allows such ghettos to exist. But did the man—instead of carrying a knife—ever try to flee the ghetto to a more humane environment? Most of this country's population is composed of the descendants of people who hated their environments in England, Europe, Russia, who fled them and survived, and even prospered. Everybody has had a choice, somewhere down the line.

The hidden agenda is a facet of the human psyche that it is not safe to leave unexplored. A woman in her sixties comes to my office in a state of angry depression. The target of her acrimony is her grown daughter, who is so wrapped in a brilliant career that she has no time for her mother. "She throws me a few crumbs, a few dinners, a few weekends a year. I never thought I would have such an ungrateful daughter!"

This was her reward for giving her daughter eighteen years of devoted motherhood, with the benefits of a fine education and the opportunities to develop her gifts. When she chose motherhood, her eyes were open to its burdens and sacrifices as well as its joys. She gave her devotion selflessly.

Selflessly? Yes, but with a string attached, a string she had never consciously examined, and that string has now grown into a rope that is nearly choking her. Her daughter is an internationally known professional woman who travels most of the year and can only squeeze into her busy life a few social occasions with her mother. But even if she were not such a successful career woman, would not the daughter be entitled to live her own life without the accusation of ingratitude and neglect? If the mother was suffering from financial need, and the daughter failed to give help that she could afford, then the accusation might have some justification. But what this mother wanted, as repayment for her devotion, was that her daughter should assuage the loneliness of her later years, that somehow she was entitled to share her daughter's life instead of living a life of her own.

This secret agenda never surfaced until many sessions of therapy. Did she give her eighteen years of devotion for a reward? She denied it indignantly. Yet, now she was angrily claiming repayment.

The secret expectations inevitably emerge to taunt us. Do the generals, the admirals, the corporation tycoons, who have drunk the intoxicating draughts of their power and high honors, step down gracefully into obscurity when they retire? Rarely. More often they smolder in rage, and bore their visitors with endless narratives of their past triumphs, which in their secret agenda they had expected would be celebrated forever. People are polite to them, but seldom bend the knee retroactively!

There comes a phase in many a teen-ager's life when it is a kind of triumph over the adult world to be as unlovable as possible. Parents cringe at their children's rude and unruly conduct, suffer their surly retorts, worry over the risks and dangers they invite. It is an American custom to make concessions to outrageous adolescent tantrums.

But I know one pair of parents who saved themselves fifteen thousand dollars in psychiatric fees. Their sixteen-year-old son had been breaking up the furniture, beating his younger brothers, and habitually violating every canon of civilized conduct as though it were his right to do so. So one day, instead of taking him to a psychiatrist, they handed him a one-way ticket to California. "Let's face it," they told him. "You don't like us and we don't like you. You don't like the way we live, so here is a ticket to another part of the country where you can live the way you like. We will send you a hundred dollars a month until you are eighteen. Phone us if you wish, and tell us how you are getting along, but don't come back!"

To the son this seemed like a good deal, and he went cheerfully. After working as a dishwasher, janitor, latrine attendant, he phoned his parents, pleading to return. They refused, saying that it would only be the same as before and they would not endure it. Three months later he phoned again—he couldn't stand it, he was going to kill himself. They were very sorry, but they still held firm. Another three months passed. He reported that he had a job that paid seventy-five dollars a week, but he hated it—couldn't he come home? They said, "With our allowance, you now have the income of a hundred dollars a week—that's fine! Please continue to enjoy the California climate until you are eighteen. Then you will no longer be our responsibility and you can do as you like."

On his eighteenth birthday he voluntarily came home and asked to rejoin the family. And also on his own volition he registered for college—which his parents agreed to pay for—and he has been a more or less normally agreeable member of the family ever since.

Were these "bad" parents, heartless monsters? As I came to know them, they were humane but tough-minded in defense of their own lives and the lives of their younger children. Here was no hidden agenda. They knew the risk of their drastic treatment, counted the possible cost in grief if their exiled son came to harm, and weighed it against the values of a civilized family life, once the unmanageable barbarian was removed.

We make choices every day, unless we are living in a coma or drifting in dreams, and usually our choices move us in a consistent direction toward a specific goal. I say that we should make the choice of our direction consciously and knowingly, instead of on the basis of a hidden agenda. And I see three choices, without judging any of them good or bad.

We can choose the world of money, prestige, and power, which beckons with material rewards, glamor, and excitement.

We can choose the world of self, insulated and isolated, whose only lines of communication are with fantasy and daydreams.

Or, we can choose the interpersonal world of the self in relationships with others and the modest rewards that love, friendship, and concern for another can bring.

Let us be warned: The roads to these three worlds do not often intersect. Each has its values. Even the world of fantasy has the value of protecting the dreamer from the challenges of reality—until he is really knocked down by a real car. And we are free to take any of these roads, provided we know the cost of the journey. It is when we take a road without knowing the toll charges we must pay at the end, that crushing difficulties can arise.

For if we choose the route of money, prestige, and power, we cannot expect to be loved for ourselves, or to experience the warmth of fellow-feeling.

And if we choose the life that feeds on fantasies, we cannot expect to attain wealth and power, or love and concern from another.

And, finally, if we choose the world of the humble humanist and shape our lives for the exchange of love and friendship, then we cannot bitch that we are not rich, powerful, glamorous, and celebrated!

We are free only when we come to realize what the costs and carrying charges are for each and every choice we make—and that no choice is wholly good or wholly bad.

Nor is it a simple matter to define what it is to be human. But we can describe its central core.

To be human is to take account of another human being, to recognize the peculiar blend of "good" and "bad" that is unique to that person. Only by taking account of another's human blend of virtues and failings do we become aware of ourselves.

Not everybody needs the help of a therapist to learn this secret of self-realization, the beginning of the art of creating true relationships. Many go on stumbling, hurting themselves and others in the dark delusive corridors of daydreaming, of magical thinking that we can reshape another in the form that we wish the other to be. But many do learn, through the trial and error of living a life. They learn to give up judgmental thinking about the "should" and "should not" of others, about what is "bad" and "good" in another's conduct, and to see only what *is*. On that basis, they have the true freedom to choose.

It was the existential philosopher Martin Heidegger's great perception that we are fully human only in relation to another human being. Apply that to daily living and it means that the road leading to that elusive self within us can only be reached by way of the other.

And there is the end of the search for identity, for what gives life its meaning, for what makes us human.

- *To find yourself through another, you don't have to move into his skin; you don't even have to like him very much.*

- *To err is human, to forgive is human.*

- *The reason virtue is not its own reward is that nobody can agree on what virtue is.*

- *We might think less about who is good and who is bad, and more about creating an emotional climate in which all our relationships can thrive as between equals.*